THE NORTHERN IRELAND PROBLEM

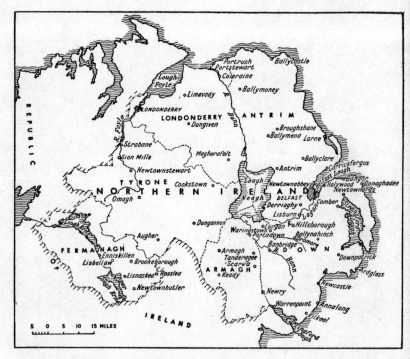

Northern Ireland, showing the more important
of the places mentioned in the text.

THE
NORTHERN IRELAND PROBLEM

A STUDY IN GROUP RELATIONS

by

DENIS P. BARRITT

and

CHARLES F. CARTER

SECOND EDITION

OXFORD UNIVERSITY PRESS

LONDON   NEW YORK   OXFORD

1972

Oxford University Press

LONDON   OXFORD   NEW YORK

GLASGOW   TORONTO   MELBOURNE   WELLINGTON

CAPE TOWN   IBADAN   NAIROBI   DAR ES SALAAM   LUSAKA   ADDIS ABABA

DELHI   BOMBAY   CALCUTTA   MADRAS   KARACHI   LAHORE   DACCA

KUALA LUMPUR   SINGAPORE   HONG KONG   TOKYO

ISBN 0 19 285058 X

© Oxford University Press 1962, 1972
First published by Oxford University Press, 1962
Reissued with a new Preface and Postscript as an
Oxford University Press paperback by Oxford University
Press, London, 1972

*Printed in Great Britain
by Redwood Press Limited, Trowbridge, Wiltshire*

FOREWORD

The Northern Ireland Problem was originally published on the initiative of this Association. When the authors undertook the study the Association appreciated their qualities of perception and human concern. The book was published in 1962 and it was accepted as a fair assessment of the problem. That judgement has strengthened with the years and the Association regards the publication as the most valuable single contribution to its aims since its foundation in 1938 by Major General Hugh Montgomery and his associates.

Much has changed since 1962 but fundamental convictions held so strongly and sincerely on both sides remain, and they have become even more fearfully divisive. Courageous and realistic reconciliation of these traditions is essential and urgent.

The Association welcomes the decision to reprint the book with a personal preface and postscript by the authors. Their assessments merit careful consideration. The Association looks for practical steps to lift our people out of the present bitterness on to an upward spiral of progress and development.

EDMOND GRACE
President
THE IRISH ASSOCIATION
FOR CULTURAL, ECONOMIC, AND SOCIAL RELATIONS
1972

CONTENTS

CONTENTS

Preface to Second Edition
DENIS P. BARRITT

EVENTS in Northern Ireland throughout the years since 1968 have made the Province newsworthy throughout the United Kingdom and beyond. Districts of Belfast and Londonderry, such as the Shankill or the Bogside, are now identifiable by many who ten years previously would have found it hard to place their parent cities. The great majority of Ulstermen would have gladly foregone such notoriety, gained at the price of violence and destruction, but we feel that a useful purpose may be served by reprinting this study of the complexities of a divided community whose problems, after fifty years of devolved rule, have still to be resolved. The picture would not be accurate without some notes of the developments during the whole of the ten years from the first publication of the book, since for five or six years the progress in good community relations outstripped the modest optimism of our conclusions. I have endeavoured to outline these events, leaving to Charles Carter the more difficult task of reviewing them in the postscript: otherwise the original text appears unaltered.

At the time of publication in 1962 the Irish Republican Army had recently called off its campaign against the so-called 'British installations' in Northern Ireland. Although causing some loss of life to policemen and creating fear and anxiety in Border areas, the campaign made little impact on the life of the Province. It provided the Unionist Government with a useful rallying call to unity, but provoked no Protestant desire for retaliation. The gunmen were largely discredited with the Catholic community, and they made little appeal to young people—in contrast, alas, with the present campaign.

The next year a change in leadership took place. Viscount Brookeborough was succeeded by his Minister of Finance, Captain Terence O'Neill. This old Etonian was judged from his record to be a liberal in approach, and he represented a break with the siege mentality of those old enough to have been involved with the 1920 settlement and the subsequent violence. Captain O'Neill ushered in no revolutionary era, but in the Stormont House of Commons on 7 October 1964 he stated 'My principal aims are . . . to make Northern Ireland economically stronger and more prosperous . . . and to build bridges between the two traditions within our community.'[1] This was the first time that reconciliation had been stated as official policy.

Considerable progress was made towards attracting industry to the Province,[2] but there was little evidence of any positive bridge-building action until January 1965 when O'Neill took the dramatic step of inviting the Taoiseach (Premier) of the Republic, then Mr. Sean Lemass, to visit Belfast, returning the visit shortly afterwards. In these days of diplomatic global travel a hundred mile journey might seem insignificant, but imprisoned by history as were both the political leaders, this small step by two men represented quite a major advance in community relations. Nationalists saw the move as an honest attempt at reconciliation, and it encouraged their leader at Stormont, Mr. Eddie McAteer, to become, for the first time, the official Leader of the Opposition. It was significant of the change of atmosphere that a couple of years later, when Mr. Lynch had taken over the leadership of the Government of the Republic, and repeated the visit, the event passed over almost without comment. At the time this appeared to augur well both for more co-operation with the Republic and for more reforms within Northern Ireland.

Although Ulster folk are not actively conscious of it, being the inhabitants of a small off-shore island in the Atlantic must have contributed to the durability of old customs, creeds, and shibboleths. Increased travel and communication has been breaking down the old ideas, a process much accelerated in the sixties, especially with the advent of ubiquitous television. No outside event contributed more to the improving of group relations than the liberalizing influence of Pope John

[1] N. Ireland *Hansard*, vol. 57, col. 2835.

[2] See Martin Wallace, *Northern Ireland, 50 Years of Self Government* (David and Charles, 1971) pp. 121–8. The writer is grateful for this clear and comprehensive survey, which forms a most useful reference work for the whole period.

XXIII and the Vatican Councils. The desire of the Catholic
clergy to maintain a strong hold over the activities of their
flocks had not helped in breaking down the division in the
community. With the wind of change blowing from the
Vatican Councils more strongly than many had dared hope,
the Church appeared to present a new image of co-operation,
and both clerics and laity were much more willing to come
forward to take part in activities in the community not specifically Catholic. Active steps were also taken to bring non-
Catholics into some Catholic sponsored organizations. This
move was pioneered by the Social Studies Conference, where
Protestant speakers had been invited since 1958, and was followed by others, notably the international thrift organization,
Credit Union.

Reciprocation from Protestant bodies came in the mid-
sixties, with the leading Protestant Churches passing resolutions
condemning religious discrimination at their annual meetings.
In 1965 it was reported in the press that a member of the
Presbyterian General Assembly called upon Presbyterians
to apologize for their attitude and actions towards the minority
in the past. The next year this same body accepted for discussion a report from one of their commissions which called
for the removal of a number of Catholic grievances in Northern
Ireland. It was the resultant picket of this Assembly by the
Rev. Ian Paisley's Free Presbyterians, and the refusal of
Paisley himself to pay a fine following a conviction arising
from the picket, which led to his first period of imprisonment.
Also at this time we began to hear of the Ulster Volunteer
Force (using the name of the gun-runners of 1914) whose
members were said to be connected with the murders of two
Catholics, and three Protestants received life sentences for one
killing. The U.V.F. was declared an illegal organization under
the Special Powers Act, and it did not go unnoticed that
this was the first time that this Act had been used against a
'Protestant' group.

There was also a steady growth of organizations promoting
conferences, discussions, and action across the religious divide.
The long standing Irish Association was joined by the Irish
Christian Fellowship, the Newman Society, the Corrymeela

Community, the Fellowship of Reconciliation, and others. A
a conference of Protestants and Catholics at the Corrymeela
Centre, Ballycastle at Easter 1966, the Prime Minister said
that the Government would stand up to noisy minorities, and
he called upon the people to 'shed the burdens of traditiona
grievances and ancient resentments'.[3] At Queen's University
the New Ireland Society provided a forum for students to
formulate new ideas for living in Ireland which were no
necessarily linked with any political party. They presented an
Oscar-like award, for three years prior to the outbreak of disturbances, to the person or organization making 'a significan
contribution during the year to the improvement of community relations in Northern Ireland'. The best examples o
co-operation were to be found where both groups came
together to work for a purpose beyond themselves, as with
the fund-raising organizations for overseas aid.

The Queen's Speech at Stormont in 1965 promised a
reorganization of local government structure, and that some
grant aid would be forthcoming for the (Catholic) Mater
Infirmorum Hospital. The *Belfast Telegraph*, under the inspiration of its Editor, the late Mr. John E. Sayers, had been
advocating moderation and reform, and towards the end o
1967 ran a professionally operated opinion poll which showed
that 16 per cent of the Catholics questioned preferred the existing constitutional position to an independent united Ireland
Another 47 per cent would have voted for a united Ireland
linked with Britain, a position preferred also by 38 per cent o
the Protestants. As the nature of this link with Britain was no
defined one must not read too much into these figures, but i
indicates a measure of flexibility whose existence is not usually
recognized. It also gives some estimate of the acceptance of the
régime by the Catholic community at this time, which, while i
was before the polarizing violence of recent years, was also
before the enactment of many reforms. There is furthermore
some correlation with an extensive survey carried out by Professor Rose some months later. He found that 15 per cent o
the Catholic population thought of themselves as 'British' and
another 5 per cent as 'Ulstermen'. Further, 22 per cent o

[3] Martin Wallace, *Drums and Guns: Revolution in Ulster* (Chapman, 1970) p. 92

Catholics questioned were in favour of supporting the existing constitutional position.[4]

There was another interesting change of emphasis during the sixties. Sparked off by intransigent Unionist local government housing policy in the Dungannon area, a 'Campaign for Social Justice in Northern Ireland' was formed. This movement sought by publication to draw attention in Great Britain to minority grievances, and gained considerable support with the British Labour Party and amongst Labour members at Westminster. Usually such propaganda had been linked with a need to unite Ireland in order to bring the desired result; this time a change of law and practice to bring Northern Ireland into line with the rest of Great Britain was demanded. Supporters of the campaign were almost all drawn from the Catholic community, and it can now be seen that it would have been beneficial if Protestants had taken part. Unless, however, they had come forward in great numbers, which would not have happened, they would have been suspect as under-cover anti-partitionists, and would have forfeited any liberalizing influence that they had with the Protestant community at large.

The beginning of 1968 represents the high-water mark of good relations. True, most of the action had come from professional and white-collar workers, but protest actions by the Rev. Paisley's followers (by no means wage-earners only) appeared to attract only extremists, and Sinn Fein and its military arm were discredited and made but little impact on the Catholic community as a whole. This was the year which had been proclaimed International Human Rights Year, and a Northern Ireland Human Rights Committee, linked with the U.K. body, spent some time investigating the Special Powers Acts. These Acts were seen as an embarrassment to the British Government, which was thereby unable to accept all the obligations of the European Convention of Human Rights. The Northern Ireland Committee was of the opinion that the 1926 Emergency Powers Act, which remains on the statute book as in the rest of the U.K., would give adequate power to the Government

[4] Richard Rose, *Governing without Consensus* (Faber, 1971) p. 208.

to deal with any violent insurrection. It would thus be possible, by repealing the Special Powers Acts, to remove a continual source of grievance to the Catholic community.

What was needed above all at this time was the enactment by the Unionist Government of a visible measure of reform. That it did not come in time was a great tragedy, for which the Province has had to pay dear. It was known that the British Premier, Mr. Harold Wilson, had been pressing Captain O'Neill to implement a reform programme, but O'Neill was obstructed by his right wing. They had been caught once by his unannounced invitation to Mr. Lemass, and were determined to curb their leader's reforming zeal. There was also a certain aloofness about the Premier; he lacked the common touch which would have enabled him to communicate with, and possibly carry with him, the 'grass roots' members of the Unionist Party.

The Catholic community was losing patience. As well as talk of human rights, unrest in many parts of the world was breaking out in demonstrations and mob violence. A Civil Rights Association, formed the previous year, organized a march in August 1968, to end at Dungannon. This was in support of an action taken by Mr. Austin Currie, the Nationalist M.P. for East Tyrone, who had squatted in a Dungannon Rural District Council house in protest against housing allocations. The next march was planned in Londonderry (for 5 October) because some members of a Derry Housing Action Committee had been given prison sentences for obstructionist action.

This demonstration proved to be the vital turning point in the campaign for reforms. The banning of the march from entering the centre of Londonderry by the Minister of Home Affairs (Mr. William Craig) transformed what would have been a small-scale leftish demonstration into a much larger and more widely supported affair. The M.P.s Mr. Eddie McAteer and Mr. Gerry Fitt agreed to head the march, which even included a number of Protestant supporters. Three British Labour M.P.s travelled over as observers. The ill-advised police order to break up what had been a peaceful demonstration with a baton charge ensured a wide television coverage, which forced the problems of Northern Ireland before the world at large.

Within five crowded weeks, on 22 November, the Government announced a package deal of reform measures. These were:

1. All local authorities were to publish a readily understood scheme for the allocation of houses.

2. An Ombudsman was to be appointed to investigate grievances in central government administration.

3. The business vote in local government elections was to be abolished forthwith, and within three years a comprehensive reform and modernization of local government would take place.[5]

4. The Special Powers Act was to be reviewed as soon as conditions allowed, and those clauses conflicting with international obligations withdrawn from use.

5. The Londonderry City Council was suspended and a Development Commission appointed for three years, charged with the advancement of industrial development and house building.

It was said at the time that Captain O'Neill had to forgo a promise of universal franchise at the next local government elections in order to gain the acceptance by his party for the appointment of the Development Commission for Londonderry. Although one may argue that the changes agreed to were overdue and that there was continuing pressure from Westminster, yet nevertheless there had been encouraging progress. Apart from some rioting in Londonderry after the 5 October action the demonstrations had remained— by design—very free from violence. This non-violent approach was found also among the students of the Queen's University, a cross-section of whom demonstrated in Belfast under the

[5] The business vote allowed a nominee vote for each £10 valuation of Limited Companies up to a maximum of six. The occupier qualification of £10 valuation (plus a vote for his wife) remained until 25 November 1969 when the Electoral Law Act (N.I. 1969) enfranchised all Northern Ireland citizens over 18 as with the Stormont provisions.

For carefully documented evidence of this period see *Disturbances in Northern Ireland*, H.M.S.O., 1969 (Cmd. 532)—the report of a three man investigation commission under the chairmanship of Lord Cameron (the 'Cameron commission').

banner of the newly formed Peoples' Democracy. This movement gradually became 'left' dominated, and invited the
participation of outside supporters. It consequently lost its
mass student appeal.

This was the moment to call a long moratorium on public
demonstrations, but once a movement has reached boiling
point it is hard to turn off the heat. There was some ugly ultra-
Protestant violence against the student marchers from Belfast
to Londonderry (chiefly at Burntollet Bridge) in January 1969,
but in general the Protestant opposition had not really become
organized in spite of the efforts of the Rev. Paisley and his
Ulster Constitution Defence Committee, supported by the Loyal
Citizens of Ulster, who had Major Bunting, a mathematics
teacher at the Belfast College of Technology, as their leader.

It was obvious, however, that continued demonstrations in
the traditional summer marching period would lead to sectarian
violence on a major scale. No one at this period had been
seriously injured, let alone killed, but past experience has
shown that once serious violence breaks out then all parties
consider that they have a just cause for grievance and redress,
the original reasons for the dispute are confused and forgotten,
and, as in war, 'truth is the first casualty'. Unfortunately,
Northern Ireland has proved no exception to this pattern,
but at this period there was still a chance for 'the groundswell
of moderate opinion' as Captain O'Neill put it, to take control.
On 8 December 1968 he took, for Northern Ireland, the
unprecedented step of appealing to the public on television.
He asked for support for a reasoned approach to reforms, and
urged an Ulster 'armed with justice' rather than with military
strength. A privately sponsored press petition received an
endorsement of 150,000 signatures for his policy.

Two organizations came into being at this period which
strengthened the support for peaceful change. One, called
PACE (Protestant and Catholic Encounter) set out to bring
Protestants and Catholics together to hear each others' points
of view. Out of dialogue they hoped for common action. A
number of branches have since been formed throughout the
Province, and the movement runs a quarterly journal. As well
as promoting conferences and discussions, the groups arrange

joint activities in youth clubs, and recreational and social welfare pursuits.

The other and larger body is the New Ulster Movement, which, as its name suggests, sets out to provide a new co-operative approach to life in Ulster. Its first rallying point was support for all pro-reform candidates in the February 1969 election. It grew rapidly in strength and at one period had some 48 branches and 10,000 members. Although it was quasi-political some members wanted to form a joint Protestant/ Catholic political party, accepting the constitutional position of Northern Ireland but with a new attitude towards the old divisions. This new Alliance Party largely grew out of the N.U.M. branches, and intends contesting all local government elections as a start, and then later to try to make itself felt at national level. In the meantime N.U.M. concentrates on acting as a reconciling body and on publishing political solutions deemed to be viable in the context of the time.[6]

When O'Neill found that the hard-line dissidents within his party had met separately and publicly declared in favour of a change in leadership he decided to test his support in the country. He fought the February 1969 election with an official manifesto calling for 'equal rights for all as a matter of principle', but his party was very divided. Some official candidates were pro-O'Neill, some were obviously right wing. There were unofficial right wing Protestant Unionists, and some unofficial pro-O'Neill reform candidates. In the event he just failed to get enough pro-reform members returned to give him the backing he needed. The Rev. Paisley's Protestant Unionists were not successful, though Paisley himself dealt O'Neill a heavy blow, by standing in the Premier's own constituency and polling 39 per cent of the votes to the Premier's 47 per cent.

The Civil Rights movement had considerable influence on the campaign and the two Derry 'Rights' leaders, Mr. John Hume and Mr. Ivan Cooper (a Protestant) were returned, Hume defeating the former leader of the Nationalists, Mr. Eddie McAteer. A student demonstrator and member of the

[6] *The Reform of Stormont*, June 1971 (advocating Proportional Representation); *The Way Forward*, November 1971 (advocating Commission rule for a period) (New Ulster Movement, 3 Botanic Avenue, Belfast).

Peoples' Democracy, Miss Bernadette Devlin, appeared as a candidate and polled more votes than many expected.[7]

There was growing opposition to Captain O'Neill among the more die-hard Protestants who mounted an 'O'Neill must go' campaign. Explosions at a reservoir, at electric pylons, and water installations took place and were at first attributed to the I.R.A., but were almost certainly U.V.F. attempts to discredit the régime. Captain O'Neill found it increasingly difficult to get any support amongst his party in the House, and faced with increasing resignations he, himself, finally resigned the leadership on 28 April. One of his last acts as Premier was to carry through the parliamentary party a motion to adopt a universal franchise (as used in parliamentary elections) in the next local government elections. It was somewhat ironical that the Unionists who had campaigned that 'O'Neill must go', now found that under the new leader, Major Chichester-Clark, they were accepting further reforms, first the principle of universal franchise, and then a Commissioner for Complaints at local government level—which was in advance of Westminster's legislation.

The question of local government franchise had been built up to an emotive rallying cry of 'one man, one vote' by the Civil Rights movement. (It must be remembered that the parliamentary franchise is the same as in Britain.) The reform meant that about 30 per cent more voters would be added to the local government electoral register—Protestants as well as Catholics—but almost certainly a greater proportion of Catholics. Without a re-drawing of electoral boundaries this would, in fact, have altered the control of very few councils. In the minds of the Civil Rights leaders the slogan meant something akin to proportional representation in local government elections, but to the less politically minded its emotional overtones suggested, to the Catholic, that the vote was being withheld from him, and to the Protestant, that it was tantamount to handing over local government control to Catholics.

[7] Miss Devlin won a by-election for the Westminster Parliament in April 1969 for the Mid-Ulster seat in a straight fight with the former member's widow (a Unionist). She campaigned for a non-sectarian socialist workers' republic of all Ireland, but won the seat as a Catholic civil rights worker—in spite of her policy rather than because of it.

The July Orange processions passed off without undue trouble, but as the traditional 12 August Apprentice Boys march in Londonderry approached, there was great tension and fear among the families in the Catholic Bogside district. This symbolic annual event commemorated the closing of the gates of the City in 1689 by a few apprentice boys while the City Fathers vacillated before the advancing army of the Catholic James the Second. In 1969 it was feared that the Orange marchers, reinforced by an enthusiastic Glasgow contingent, would invade the Bogside. Plans were made to evacuate some children, and stones and petrol bombs were prepared in readiness. In the event the behaviour of the Apprentice Boys was exemplary but the tension was such that the Bogside youths foolishly approached the marchers to jeer and throw stones. The police put up with it for a while and then charged the stone throwers, driving them back into the Bogside. They then came within range of the prepared ammunition and the battle of the Bogside was on, the inhabitants not forgetting that earlier in the year some police had entered the area and run amok. In an attempt to divert attention from Londonderry, stones and petrol bombs were thrown at police stations in various other towns in the Province, including Belfast. Here widespread rioting developed on 14 and 15 August and there were numerous confrontations between the police and rioters who started fires in business premises. Behind the police came Protestant mobs who systematically burnt whole streets of houses. In a few days of rioting in the city five Catholics and two Protestants were shot and 270 houses completely burnt (together with a similar number damaged), the great majority of which were occupied by Catholics. At this point Major Chichester-Clark requested the help of the British Army. This was welcomed by Catholics (in contradiction to the traditional anti-British attitude) because they felt that they could not trust the police, who had failed to give them protection.

The Prime Minister went to London and on 19 August 1969 a joint communiqué was issued, which became known as the Downing Street Declaration. The ultimate responsibility of the British Government for law and order was stressed, and the provision of troops on a temporary basis confirmed. The two Governments then declared that 'every citizen of Northern Ireland is entitled to the same equality of treatment and freedom from discrimination as obtains in the rest of the United Kingdom, irrespective of political views or religion.'

Another communiqué announced that General Sir Ian Freeland would assume overall command, not only of the Army but of the Ulster Special Constabulary also. The two Governments were to discuss as a matter of urgency the civilian security services. A three man advisory body headed by Lord Hunt was set up to report on police structure.[8] It reported on 3 October and shortly afterwards its main recommendations were implemented. These were to relieve the police of all riot duties and to limit their carrying of arms. Special efforts were to be made to increase the force above the existing strength of about 3,000, and in particular to try to recruit Catholics and so increase the numbers to more than their existing proportion of 12 per cent or so. The 'B' Special police (see p. 62) were to be stood down and replaced by a part-time Ulster Defence Regiment within the British Army.

In the meantime the Home Secretary, Mr. James Callaghan, had visited Northern Ireland. He walked in the riot areas and talked to all and sundry. It was for him a personal triumph, and he did much to restore a feeling of some confidence in a badly shaken Province. When speaking in public he was careful to stress that all reforms proposed had been jointly agreed and would be carried out by the Northern Ireland Government, but it was difficult not to believe that the impetus had come from the British Government and that the Stormont representatives had no option but to agree. A number of new measures were announced in further joint communiqués made on 29 August and 10 October 1969 as follows:

1. One central housing authority would be set up to take over the tasks of local authorities and the Northern Ireland Housing Trust.

2. A Ministry of Community Relations was to be formed, and also an independent Community Relations Commission.

[8] *Report of the Advisory Cttee. on Police in Northern Ireland*, H.M.S.O., October 1969 (Cmd. 535).

3. The appointment of a local government commissioner for complaints was confirmed.

4. Universal suffrage in local government elections was confirmed, and it was decided to set up a review body to re-examine the local government proposals. This body, composed of three Protestants and three Catholics, under the chairmanship of Mr. Patrick Macrory, was appointed on 17 December 1969, and reported on 29 May 1970 (Cmd. 546). The reduction of the number of local authorities from the original 73 to 26 District Councils was recommended. In general the findings were accepted by Stormont in January 1971. A Boundaries Commissioner was then appointed, under the Local Government Boundaries Act, to delineate the 26 areas in readiness for the local government elections in the Autumn of 1972.

5. It was decided to bring in a Bill to curb incitement to hatred, and this measure reached the statute book on 2 July 1970.[9]

6. Some attempt was made to prevent discrimination in employment in the public sector by requiring all public bodies to adopt an approved code of employment procedure, and by requiring an anti-discrimination clause to be introduced into all government contracts.[10] A working party was set up to study the formation of a Public Service Commission to look into certain aspects of local government and Civil Service staffing. Consideration of action to prevent discrimination in private employment was promised, but nothing has so far emerged in this more complicated field.

On 27 August 1969 a Tribunal was established to investigate the August riots. Under the chairmanship of Mr. Justice Scarman it had power to subpoena witnesses. The evidence was of massive proportions, and the report was not published until April 1972.

[9] *Incitement to Hatred Act (Northern Ireland)*, July 1970.

[10] It was not until 22 June 1971 that this provision came into force. For an official account of the reform measures see *A Record of Constructive Change*, August 1971 (Cmd. 558).

Back in the Autumn of 1969 the chief problem was to get the homeless housed and to cope with the new problem of intimidation, which made the whole position much more serious. The events of the summer had been a bad shock to the morale of both Protestants and Catholics, as it suggested a return to the 'troubles' of the twenties, something which would have been unthinkable a year or so previously. There was now widespread fear, kept alive by despicable and cowardly intimidation (usually anonymous) of families to 'get out or else . . .'. The sufferers were both Protestant and Catholic families who found themselves living in an area where the other group dominated. Those of mixed marriage were not wanted by either group, and at times moved from one area to another only to find fresh abuse and insults, directed this time at the other partner.

On the other hand in certain sectors of the city where the population was mixed Peace Committees sprang up *ad hoc*, staffed by citizens from both sides who were well known in the area, pledged to stop rioting wherever possible and to protect any minorities within their area against intimidation. They were often joined by the local clergy, who with others were commonly present in the streets at 'closing time' to break up any gangs which might become potential dangers to the peace of the neighbourhood. The Peace Committees were linked together by a central body. As the immediate danger of a civil war receded these Committees lost their impetus, and when serious rioting broke out a year later were unable to exert an influence, for the nature of the conflict had altered and the gunmen were in control.

The statutory housing authorities found it a considerable strain trying to house the displaced and homeless at a time when they needed all available accommodation to make possible extensive re-development plans in the city. These plans were held up as large numbers took the law into their own hands and squatted in new or even partly completed houses and flats. Grants paid by the Supplementary Benefits Commission to those whose homes had been destroyed were augmented by money subscribed to a fund set up by the *Belfast Telegraph*. This 'Innocent Victims Fund' amounted to £66,000 and to this the British Government added £250,000. The

Stormont Government had provided over £50,000 for additional first aid relief, and these funds were administered by Church bodies and voluntary organizations.

In the Catholic areas of the Bogside in Londonderry and the Falls in Belfast streets were barricaded off and the police were not accepted. The Army did not at first remove the barricades, a fact that was much resented in Protestant areas. Amongst Protestant workers there was much confusion and resentment. There was a feeling that the Unionist Government, whom they had always been taught to trust as a bulwark against Nationalism and against Catholics in general, was letting them down. The British Government, to which also they had given allegiance, was giving in to the demands of the 'Fenians', and had stripped them of the protection of the arms of the R.U.C. and of the 'B' Specials. The substitute, the British Army, they argued, though once invincible, now let the Queen's enemies do what they wanted—enemies whose views appeared to be supported by television interviews. The feeling of insecurity, particularly in the Shankill district, was intensified as they saw their familiar landmarks, and indeed whole streets, vanishing to make way for new development, and they found that the first blocks of new flats at the city end of their area were being filled with Catholic families. It was not so paradoxical, therefore, that the people of this area should come into violent confrontation with the Army and that the first citizens to be shot by the Army should be two Protestants from the Shankill district.

Eventually the barricades came down, but the Falls still remained a 'no go' area for the police and the inhabitants were thus left unprotected against the ordinary criminal who profited from looting from abandoned homes.

General Freeland had spoken soon after the arrival of the Army about the honeymoon period of acceptance being of limited duration, but during the winter of 1969 the presence of the Army did ensure a period of uneasy calm, uneasy in that there were many reports of the build-up of secret arms stores by both sides. Great restraint was shown by the Army in dealing with sporadic rioting and confrontations of groups, and later in dealing with the activities of youths, throwing stones and petrol bombs.

In April 1970 a hitherto unaffected Catholic housing area, Ballymurphy, took exception to a Scottish regiment stationed near by as it was deemed to be anti-Catholic. Rioting followed, but, although there were shots fired, on the whole it was of the youthful hooligan type. Indeed on one notable occasion a riot was prevented by a group of mothers linking arms and forming a cordon across the road.

Although it was known that there had been a split for some time in the I.R.A., little had been heard of either wing and their presence in the North had not really been felt. The first real taste of their potential power was felt at the end of June in East Belfast, where the Provisional I.R.A. gunmen were active. The official I.R.A. had accepted a full revolutionary socialist policy. They were anti-clerical and hoped to unite all Irish workers in an independent workers' republic. In contrast to these 'red' I.R.A. the Provisionals were the 'green' army, extreme nationalist republicans intent only in getting the British out and removing the border. Paradoxically they were willing at this time to accept direct British rule in the belief that it would lead to the ending of partition.

The Army began to get worried about the mounting stores of weapons and at the beginning of July instigated searches in the densely populated narrow streets of the Lower Falls area, although the priests in the district warned that this would lead to trouble. The Army met with serious opposition, and they sealed off the whole area and imposed a curfew. After several days of fighting, ten people had been killed and much damage to property caused. C.S. gas had been used and this had led to much distress in households trapped in their homes.

Though hard-line Protestants were pleased at this show of force, this was the real turning of the road and the beginning of the alienation of whole Catholic areas from the Army. Even though many Catholics did not like the I.R.A., they resented having their homes searched, and came to look upon the Army as the tool of the Stormont Government, which now appeared to be dragging its feet on the reform programme. The hard-line element in the Unionist Party seemed to be gaining strength, and in by-elections the Rev. Paisley and a fellow Free Presbyterian, the Rev. William Beattie, were elected to Stormont. On the Catholic side the return of the Conservative Party to power in June 1970 at Westminster in place of Labour was thought to be the reason for the hardening of the Army's attitude. Catholic feelings were not assuaged by the passing of the Criminal Justice (Temporary Provisions) Act (N.I.), which imposed a mandatory prison sentence for such a wide list of offences 'committed during the period of the present emergency' that it covered ordinary breaches of the peace not related to the disturbances, and later had to be modified.

Some measures calculated to improve group relations had been enacted. A Community Relations Ministry was formed, a small team headed by a minister of cabinet rank. This was backed by a Community Relations Commission, independent of the Government, under the chairmanship of Dr. Maurice Hayes, himself a Catholic. (He resigned in 1972.) He had a director and a team of field officers whose task it was to promote and encourage community action throughout the Province. The Commissioner for Complaints at Local Government level, Mr. J. M. Benn, a former Permanent Secretary to the Ministry of Education, made his first report. During 1970 he received 1,193 complaints, and although maladministration was found in 14 of the 125 cases examined under this heading, in another 14 cases where religious or political discrimination was alleged the Commissioner found no allegations proved.

In March 1971 Major Chichester-Clark, worried by the continual pressures from his right wing, resigned, and Mr. Brian Faulkner took over. In the past he had been regarded as anti-Catholic, but he now accepted the principles of the reform programme and it was felt that of his party he was the most likely, with his political acumen, to hold the country together. He showed that he was willing to make experiments by appointing a former Northern Ireland Labour Party M.P., Mr. David Bleakley, to the post of Minister of Community Relations, with full cabinet rank, for the maximum stipulated period for a co-opted person of six months. In 1971 he appointed Dr. G. B. Newe, the Secretary of the Northern Ireland Council of Social Service, as Minister of State, again for a six month period. It was thought that Dr. Newe, a Catholic, could keep the Cabinet informed as to the tenor of Catholic opinion in the Province.

After the August 1969 riots, both sides claimed that the courts were biased against their own group. Catholics, in particular, felt that the fact that the police acted as public prosecutors meant that there was a natural built-in bias. In April 1971 the Government accepted a recommendation that there should be a Department of Public Prosecutions set up to take this responsibility out of the hands of the police, and bring the practice more nearly into line with the rest of the United Kingdom.

These actions were not sufficient to turn the swelling tide of violence. Although many towns in Northern Ireland were free from disturbance of any kind, the communities in the city of Belfast became more and more segregated in daily living, and the people more polarized in their attitudes. A new hazard was added in 1971 to the hooligan's petrol bomb and the sniper's bullet; this was the gelignite bomb. Apart from the danger to life and the damage to property, continued bomb scares had a disrupting effect on business, interrupting production and deterring shoppers from coming into the centre of the city. The long land boundary with the Republic, which it was almost impossible to patrol, allowed not only a relatively easy access for arms and explosives, but also a sanctuary for escaping guerrillas. The fact that Mr. Lynch had not taken the same strong action against the I.R.A. as did his predecessor against illegal movements during the 1956–62 campaign (see p. 134) caused bitter feeling in the North and made talks with the Republic more difficult.

An imaginative political step was needed, and it seemed that the Premier had provided this when he stated in the House of Commons that his Government aimed at 'governing with the consent and acceptance of a far wider majority than was constituted by those who elected the governing party': it must be made possible 'for all responsible elements in the community to play a constructive part in its institutions'.[11] Three influential committees were to be added to the existing Public Accounts Committee, to consider government policies on social services, industrial development, and environmental matters. Further, it was proposed that the opposition should provide the salaried chairmen for two of these committees.

[11] N. Ireland *Hansard*, vol. 82, col. 26.

These proposals were well received by opposition members, a number of whom were now grouped into the Social Democratic and Labour Party. It was ironical and tragic that within a few weeks of this move, when a real breakthrough towards greater participation by the minority seemed to have been achieved, the whole of the opposition (save for Mr. F. V. Simpson, the Northern Ireland Labour Party member) was to withdraw from the House and propose setting up a separate Parliament.

The decision to withdraw arose out of an incident in the Bogside. During one of the many riots in this area, two civilians were shot by the Army and mortally wounded. The Army claimed they were handling weapons; the Bogsiders denied this and called for an investigation. Mr. John Hume, the member for the area, realizing that unless he took action he would lose credibility with these his constituents, and allow the I.R.A. to assume control completely, hastily called together the members of the S.D.L.P. It was agreed to present a call for an inquiry into the incident as an ultimatum to the British Home Secretary—failing satisfaction they would withdraw from Stormont. When the request was turned down they withdrew, and other nationalistically inclined members followed suit.

Due to sectarian loyalties and the very real fear of reprisals, it was proving almost impossible to get witnesses to give evidence against captured gunmen. Bombing incidents were increasing, and Mr. Faulkner was under pressure from his right wing to take sterner measures. On 9 August 1971 he announced the reactivation of internment and that some 300 men had been taken for questioning. It was understood that the Army was not in favour of this move, and certainly the immediate result was to spark off new riots and to intensify the gelignite bombing campaign.[12] The leading Protestant Churches quickly

[12] 1971	Soldiers killed (including Ulster Defence Regiment)	R.U.C. killed	Civilians killed (not incl. I.R.A.)	No. of incidents	Bombs	
					lb. exploded	lb. dismantled by Army
Jan.–March	6	2	11	209	510	120
April–July	4	–	4	476	1650	670
August	7	–	28	207	960	270
Sept.–Dec.	31	9	71	800	6477	1740

Source—*Fortnight*, 12 January 1972 (derived from Army press releases).

came out in support of internment, possibly because they saw it as a rapid means of curbing violence and loss of life. Moderates in the Catholic community warned that internment would alienate whole areas and drive them into the hands of the I.R.A. The position was not improved by stories of brutal treatment during interrogation. Although 'physical brutality' was not admitted in an official inquiry,[13] methods used during questioning in depth, it was thought, did constitute physical ill-treatment, and their publication caused considerable disquiet in the United Kingdom. The continuation of internment and of allegations of brutality has alienated a very large proportion of the Catholic community, and strengthened the hands of their leaders in refusing to negotiate until internment is ended. The deaths in a Londonderry demonstration on 30 January 1972 also had a profound effect.

Protestant opinion was equally enraged by the intensifying of terrorist activity, particularly indiscriminate bombing in towns and cities leading to the death and maiming of citizens going about their daily business. A right wing workers' movement, Vanguard, emerged, led by Mr. William Craig, holding mass rallies, and hinting at U.D.I. if strong action was not taken. Clearly an impasse had been reached and the initiative rested with Westminster. When the British Government eventually proposed taking complete control of security in Northern Ireland, Mr. Faulkner resigned, and the Stormont Parliament was prorogued on 30 March 1972.

This then is the sad history of the decline from a promising era of co-operation into a state of near civil war. Many features of the new situation arise from facts described in this book. The postscript attempts to look at present problems in a more general way.

[13] *Report of the enquiry into allegations against the security forces of physical brutality in N. Ireland arising out of events on the 9 August 1971* (under the chairmanship of Sir Edmund Compton), H.M.S.O., 1971 (Cmd. 4823).

INTRODUCTION

THIS BOOK is written at a time when, under the stress of the great division of East and West which threatens all human civilization, men are more willing to look again at lesser causes of difference. Thus the countries of Western Europe are bringing into effect their plans for economic unity, which must imply some degree of political unity also; and within the divided Christian Church, leaders are increasingly willing to emphasize the points of unity instead of the reasons for division. These are strong movements of opinion which must have their effect, even within the small territory of Northern Ireland; yet to those who live there the tension between Protestants and Catholics[1] seems to be a cause of disunity so ancient and all-pervading that a change is difficult to imagine. In politics, in education, in business, in social life, and in recreation, strong forces tend to place a man according to the church with which he worships—in the Ulster phrase, according to which foot he digs with. There is no assurance that the divisions are becoming less with the passage of time; on the contrary, a divided education and a divided social and political life tend to deepen and confirm the fundamental cleavage. That cleavage is, of course, much more than a difference of theology, for the differences of religion run alongside differences of race and of historical origin. The Catholic community gathers to itself the memories of an oppressed nation, the pride of a remote Celtic past before the Norman invaders came, the bitterness of a people leaderless and dispossessed at the time of the Plantations. The Protestant community has its own proud memories of the struggle for freedom of conscience at Derry and the Boyne, of high principles successfully maintained, of ordered and productive agriculture and industry brought to an undeveloped land, of an ascendancy held by constant vigilance, enterprise, and hard work.

[1] We recognize the strong feeling of many Protestants that they are 'Catholic' in the proper sense of the word; but we hope that they will excuse us for using the word here to mean 'Roman Catholic', for it would be awkward to use the full title many hundreds of times in this book. In Northern Ireland the word 'Protestant' is synonymous with 'non-Roman-Catholic'.

In fact, the differences are so many and profound that they leave
an impression of a problem which is eternal and without hope.
English people often find it difficult to understand that there can
be any present-day relevance in what people believe about the
happenings of 1641 or 1690, or even those of 1912. But the past
can still have a lively influence on Irish thought, and, though the
passage of time may turn history into mythology, there is little
sign that it will bring forgetfulness of old battles and old wrongs.

There is, however, another side to the matter. The two communities in Northern Ireland live side by side, generally at peace.
Their people are linked by many ties of personal friendship, and by
occasional significant ventures in co-operation. Furthermore, it
would be wrong to suppose that divisions and tensions make
Northern Ireland an unhappy or neurotic land; on the whole,
people manage to adapt themselves very well to ancient and
continuing differences, and they use those differences to add to the
richness and humour of life.

But the differences undoubtedly lead to frustration and insecurity, which affect political, economic, and social development.
Therefore, there are in both communities people who consider
that however hopeless and eternal the problem appears, it must
be solved. The present study was sponsored at the beginning of
1959 by a group of such people, the Northern Committee of the
Irish Association for Cultural, Economic, and Social Relations.
The first two of the aims of this Association are:

'To foster through the initiative of its individual members more
neighbourly relations between those Irish people who differ from each
other in politics and religion.

'To encourage respect for the convictions of others, to correct
misrepresentation and to expose intolerance and intimidation.'

It seemed to the Committee that it would be wise to find out
just what the problem is, and to look at the points of conflict and
of co-operation in the dispassionate and impartial light of truth.
The sturdy controversialists of each side are very ready to set up a
conventional image of their opponents, so that they may knock it
down; but the image has often become little like reality. There is,
in fact, widespread ignorance about what 'the other side' believes,
does, and feels. The Committee considered that it would be no

bad thing if the fires of controversy were to be stoked with a few facts, which commonly provide a much less combustible material than fancies.

The main purpose, then, was to take some of the heat out of controversy, and to help reasonable men to think about the problems of a divided community in a reasonable way. The Irish Association does not hope thereby to 'solve the Irish problem', but (by this book and in many other ways) to exert a little influence in favour of goodwill and co-operation. The Association hopes, however, that the book may have an interest to many who have no concern with Irish affairs, for it is a study of some parts of a singularly fascinating problem in sociology. Here are racial, religious, political, economic, and social conflicts all rolled into one; here, on Britain's doorstep, are two communities which live apart, even to the extent of playing different games. There may be a wider interest in discovering how society adapts itself to such a continuing division.

The authors of this book, however, are not dispassionate observers from Mars. We both have a profound love for the land and people of Northern Ireland; one of us (D.P.B.) has lived there most of his life, though the other (C.F.C.) stayed for only eight years. Both of us being Quakers, we stand a little outside the main Protestant tradition, in a body whose nature was strongly influenced by persecutions which in the seventeenth century it shared with both Dissenters and Catholics. But we are, of course, 'Protestant' in the sense in which that term is always used in Northern Ireland—that is to say, we do not recognize the author-ity of the Bishop of Rome. We do not pretend to know all the ways in which we may be biased or blind to reality; we can only do our best to be fair and honest.

It is necessary to make it clear that this book is about *Northern Ireland* only. The division of the country, now forty years old, has left the problems of Protestant ascendancy over a large Catholic minority in the North, and of Catholic ascendancy over a small Protestant minority in the South. These are different (though of course related) problems; we think it better to stick to one of them. We must make it clear, also, that the title of this book is not meant to imply that Northern Ireland has only a single problem. The sectarian problem is often at the front of people's minds, but economic difficulties are equally fundamental. English readers may need to be reminded that a very high proportion of people in Northern Ireland have a definite church connexion, and indeed that they actually go to church on Sunday (see page 21). Perhaps as a result of the tension between the communities, there is little room to be indifferent about religion; Ireland is a Christian country in a sense which England can no longer claim.

We have to acknowledge the help of a great many people; the members of the Northern Committee of the Irish Association, and in particular those who guided the project; those who contributed to a special appeal for the support of the work; those who patiently answered questions and gave advice; and those who criticized and corrected chapters submitted to them for comment. Above all we are grateful for the constant support and interest of Sir Graham Larmor, President of the Irish Association. For the shortcomings and errors of the book we take full responsibility. In particular, we must make it quite clear that phrases such as 'we think that . . .' refer to the views of the authors and not necessarily of the Committee.

D. P. BARRITT
C. F. CARTER

Belfast and Manchester
December 1961

A NOTE ON ARRANGEMENT AND METHOD

WE have taken in turn the main areas of life in Northern Ireland in which conflict or co-operation can be seen at work, such as the social groupings, the educational system, employment and emigration, the social services, political life, the provision for leisure. These are interrelated, and in order to understand any of them it is necessary to know something of the historical background. We have, therefore, set at the front of the book a chapter which is about history; but we have not attempted the impossible task of summarizing Irish history in a chapter, for what is relevant is not so much what actually happened, but what people (of different outlook) think important in history. Behind all that we describe lie the differences in theology, Church government and tradition between the Catholic and the Protestant Churches; these we have in general had to leave to be understood by the reader's general knowledge, for they would require a whole library of books. We have, however, in Chapter 2 said something about the attitude of the Churches to each other. Chapters 3 and 4 deal in a broad way with the political and social background, while the succeeding chapters take up the study of particular points of conflict or co-operation. Chapter 11 sets out our main conclusions.

Our method of work was as follows. We first reviewed the whole field with the help of a sub-committee. From this review there followed innumerable suggestions for people to be interviewed and lines to be followed; and we tried (for each section) to see how far we could get by assembling existing factual information, whether published or available from reliable and expert witnesses. We were thus able to identify areas which needed additional detailed study—for instance, the relation between occupation and religion; and for these we devised special field surveys, especially in the towns of Newry and Portadown, so far as our limited resources allowed. Readers will understand that, in the situation of tension existing in Northern Ireland, we were usually asked to conceal details which would identify our informants. Such authority as our findings possess, therefore, must rest on our having drawn a picture which Ulstermen[1] recognize as broadly true, rather than on a long series of footnotes.

The field work and interviews were undertaken by one of us (D.P.B.), who was able to give over two years full-time to the project. The other author (C.F.C.) checked the conclusions against his own collection of information and helped to write the first drafts of the chapters; we then submitted the drafts to members of the sub-committee, or to outside experts, for comment. The second drafts were then prepared and approved as fit for publication.

Our material was mostly collected during 1959 and 1960. In so far as it is statistical, we have brought it up to date and checked it as carefully as we can; but the reader will see from the text that some of the statistics are meant to illustrate rather than to prove.

[1] Strictly speaking, Ulster includes the counties of Cavan, Donegal, and Monaghan, but we use the term loosely to refer to the six counties of Northern Ireland.

CHAPTER 1

TWO VIEWS OF HISTORY

THE Protestant community in Northern Ireland has both Irish and British loyalties. The outward signs of British loyalty—the flags, the patriotic speeches, the evidence of devotion to the Queen —are much more apparent than in Britain itself. When a Northern Ireland Protestant uses the word 'we' in relation to some national issue he often means 'we in the United Kingdom . . .'; he may sometimes mean 'we in Northern Ireland . . .' (for in forty years the Province has become a real object of loyalty); but he will not often mean 'we in the two parts of Ireland'. Nevertheless there remains a love of things Irish, a sense of being neither Scots nor English; in older people one sometimes finds a nostalgia for an Ireland united under Protestant domination; and there are even a few Protestants whose desire for a united Ireland would overcome their doubts about Catholic supremacy.

The Catholic community has, of course, a dominant Irish loyalty which is sometimes strongly anti-British. But anti-British sentiment is not by any means universal; some Catholics are ready to say (though more often in private than in public) that they value the United Kingdom connexion. It would be unconventional for a Catholic to admit a loyalty to Northern Ireland rather than to all Ireland, but such a loyalty is not unknown; it may be traced in a tendency to run down the unpractical activities of 'those people down South'.

The complex pattern of loyalties is a result of many events of past history, and the purpose of this chapter is to suggest which of them have been most important in creating the present condition of Northern Ireland, and how real or imagined features of the past shape the present beliefs of the two communities. It would be false, of course, to suppose that there is anything so simple as 'a Protestant view' and 'a Catholic view' of history. One must speak in terms of probabilities. It is probable that a Protestant, even of little schooling, will 'know' that freedom of religious expression was won at the Battle of the Boyne, though he will probably not know that the Pope is thought to have favoured King William's cause. It is probable that a Catholic will 'know' about Wolfe Tone and the rebellion of 1798, though he may forget that the societies of United Irishmen were Protestant in origin.

As far back as history can be traced or legend interpreted, Ireland has seen invasions of population from overseas. One of these invasions, that of the Gaels (who began to come from Gaul about the first century B.C.), was in the long run successful; that is to say, the Gaelic ruling class not only exercised economic ascendancy and political power over the previous inhabitants, imposing their own language and legal system, but also assimilated them so that the culture of previous societies became lost in the mists of legend. The Vikings, the Normans, the Scots, and the English were never so successful. The Gaelic conquest took five or six centuries, and the assimilation of previous cultures much longer, the process being especially slow in the North. But when it was substantially complete, there was created an Irish culture which is still the point of reference for those who want to emphasize the unity of the island, and its difference from the outside world.

Ireland was not in any modern sense a political unity. It was a loose structure of small states, each governed by a chief chosen from its ruling family. Some rulers exercised a nominal overlordship as provincial 'kings', and from about the fifth century the Kings of Tara claimed the status of 'High King of Ireland', exacting tribute or hostages from the provincial kings, though without much influence on local administration. But the cultural unity of Ireland was enhanced by the flowering of Christian influence, at a time when in neighbouring countries Christianity was in confusion and retreat with the breakdown of Roman order. From the fifth to the eighth centuries the 'island of saints and scholars' helped to conserve the knowledge which was being destroyed elsewhere by barbarian invasions, and sent out a stream of learned and saintly men to advance and maintain the Christian cause in Britain and in Europe.

The Norse invaders of the ninth and tenth centuries failed to establish any lasting supremacy, being finally checked at the Battle of Clontarf in 1014. Their legacy was the creation of seaport towns and the quickening of seaborne commerce; the Norse settlers were in time assimilated, but their depredations had greatly weakened the Irish monasteries and schools. The internal politics of the country remained highly confused, with much local warfare between contending chiefs. In this warfare provincial kings had already used the Norsemen as allies; it was inevitable that in time someone would call in help from across the Irish Sea, especially as by the twelfth century the skills of war were more highly developed there.

Accordingly in 1166 Dermot MacMurragh, King of Leinster, obtained from Henry II permission to recruit auxiliaries among the marcher lords of South Wales; and on his death one of these allies, Richard de Clare, called Strongbow (who had married Dermot's daughter), seized and held Leinster. This opened up a prospect of Norman barons strengthening their independence by seizing Irish territory, and the King intervened. He did so with papal approval, for the Irish Church had diverged from the traditions of Western Christendom, and the Pope considered that a strong secular power would help reformers to bring it back into line. In 1171 Henry II landed with a considerable army, and obtained recognition of his lordship from the Normans and from many of the native Irish rulers; he kept the Norse towns under his personal control.

On one view, this event represents the beginning of 750 years of subjection to British rule. This, however, involves reading into it a significance which belongs to later history. The Norman barons were alien rulers of the Anglo-Saxons as well as of the Irish; in England the distinction between the invaders and the conquered was gradually forgotten, and in Ireland the same might have happened, if the Normans had been strong and united enough to maintain order. But in the constant warfare between the barons, the Irish rulers retained their chance of power, and the opportunity to maintain Irish laws and customs in place of the feudal laws of England. By the mid-fourteenth century, the English King had little control in Ulster or Connaught, and in a defensive reaction the Norman or English settlers tried to hold what they could through a policy of *apartheid*. In the Statutes of Kilkenny of 1366 England tried to prevent the intermingling of the races, lest the native Irish influence should prevail. The policy was incapable of being carried out thoroughly, but it tended to maintain the segregation of English and Irish clergy in the Church, and

B

therefore the distinction between English and Irish Church traditions and methods of organization.

During the next two centuries the intermingling of races went on, and the great Anglo-Irish families, allied with native Irish rulers, often adopted an independent attitude which might have been the foundation of a new Irish political system. The culmination of the process came in the rise of the Earls of Kildare, who dominated much of the eastern part of the country for half a century after 1470. But these great nobles were potentially a threat to the English political system; it was a Kildare who crowned Lambert Simnel in Dublin as 'Edward VI', in opposition to the claims of Henry VII, and there were later dangers from the attempt to bring in Perkin Warbeck. In the long run, the King had to exert his authority to defend his own position; and, after various attempts, the decisive step was taken by Henry VIII in 1534. He broke the power of the Kildares, had himself proclaimed King of Ireland in 1541, and sought by conciliation to bring the Irish and the Anglo-Irish families into submission to orderly rule.

On a Protestant view, subsequent events are the inevitable working out of a tragedy. The power of England was necessarily involved in Ireland, but it was never exerted with sufficient vigour to break the ancient traditions of warfare between families; and the Reformation, though at first meeting with little resistance, was never carried through to success, so that in time the division of English from Irish became also a religious division. By the time the failure of political and religious policy became apparent, England felt a responsibility for the Protestants of Ireland, who were mainly of English origin; and she had not yet learnt to recognize that the support of colonial minorities leads to an untenable position. She sought to strengthen her position by settling more English Protestants in the country, and she was driven by attack to severe measures of repression against the native Irish, who were now a source of danger because of their loyalty to Rome and the intrigues of foreign powers. A Catholic view, however, will see in the events which followed 1534 the working out of a concept of racial superiority which reserved power and privilege to the English and the Protestants, which dispossessed many of the Irish, and which suppressed legitimate expressions of discontent with the utmost brutality.

In Ulster the settlement of Henry VIII soon broke down, and Shane O'Neill continued the traditions of the warlike Gaelic rulers by fighting the O'Donnells and the Scottish MacDonnells. He was overthrown in 1567, and the centre of trouble moved to Munster, where a rebellion in 1579–83 received Spanish help, and thus confirmed the English fears that Ireland would be used as an instrument of the policy of other powers. Thus when in 1598 Hugh O'Neill (who had raised an insurrection in the North, and had obtained much support in other parts of the country) defeated Sir Henry Bagenal's forces in battle, the government of Elizabeth took vigorous action, for they feared the renewed intervention of Spain. This indeed came in 1601, but it came too late; the English forces under Mountjoy had established too strong a hold, and had steadily eroded the O'Neill's strength. He submitted to James I in 1603, and with this act the last hope of the re-establishment of the old Gaelic social order was destroyed. In 1607 the O'Neill, Earl of Tyrone, together with Rory O'Donnell, Earl of Tyrconnell, set sail from Lough Swilly for the Continent, accompanied by many dependants.

This 'flight of the Earls' was treated as treason, and their estates (covering the four western counties of Northern Ireland, together with Cavan and Donegal) were declared forfeit to the Crown. Most of the Irish landlords who had held land under Tyrone and Tyrconnell were dispossessed, and land was handed over to 'undertakers' who agreed to bring in British settlers. There is no evidence of whether the intentions of the Earls were in fact treasonable; from the Catholic point of view, the Plantations of Ulster can be seen as an act of indiscriminate vengeance affecting Irish landlords who had done no wrong. From the contemporary Protestant point of view, the flight could be interpreted as an attempt to recruit help abroad, and as evidence that there would never be peace until the old Gaelic order had been wholly uprooted. Present-day Protestants may prefer to withhold judgement on these issues, but will see no reason why their right to be in Ireland should be questioned because of an event which took place 350 years ago.

The Plantation of Ulster was only a partial success as a means of displacing population, since there were never enough settlers to fill the land, and it was, therefore, necessary to retain Irish tenants.

It was, however, reinforced by the inflow of Scots and English into Antrim and Down, where a piecemeal process of confiscation and resettlement went on. Thus there was built up a body of men filled with hatred because they had been dispossessed; in 1641 the Irish rose against the colonists throughout Ulster, and for a time swept away the Plantation, except for a few towns such as London-derry. The 'massacres of 1641' have long remained a bitter memory for Protestants. The rebellion spread southwards, being joined by many of the Catholic gentry of Anglo-Irish stock. In the succeed-ing years the struggle was complicated by the influence of the Civil War in England; and when Cromwell landed in Ireland in 1649 his action can be seen as part of his fight against the Royalists. But he also came full of a hard religious zeal to avenge the massacres of 1641 by an equally ruthless and undiscriminating cruelty. The Cromwellian settlement dispossessed many more of the Catholic landlords throughout Ireland, and replaced them by Protestants. Thus the new order, in which social and political power was decisively in the hands of the Protestants, remains associated by many people with the hated memory of Cromwell's revenge.

It is clear that in the mid-seventeenth century Protestant settlers, at least outside the larger towns, must have felt exceedingly insecure; their very lives depended on the continued protection of English forces. At this time, therefore, the lines of division of the population into two communities became more definitely drawn, and drawn in a way which corresponded with the religious division. To the Protestant, the fact that a man was a Catholic was prima facie evidence that he would be disaffected and disloyal to the State: to the Catholic the fact that a man was a Protestant suggested that he was an alien invader maintained by foreign military power.

The fears of the Protestant community were renewed during the later years of Charles II, by evidence of favour to Catholics, and were inflamed by the accession of James II. Under the Lord Lieutenant Richard Talbot, created Earl of Tyrconnell, an active policy of restoring Catholic influence was pursued. In 1688, how-ever, James fled from England; he now hoped to use Ireland as his base for recovering power, and in March 1689, he landed at Kinsale. A Parliament which met in Dublin in May justified the

Protestant fears by passing an Act confiscating the estates of over 2,000 Protestant landlords. James in the meantime was trying to restore his authority in Ulster, which had declared for William and Mary, and he spent fifteen weeks in the futile attempt to reduce the city of Londonderry. The privations of this siege, and the joys of relief by an English naval force, have remained deeply etched on the Protestant consciousness ever since. An English force reached Ulster in August 1689, and after an inconclusive period the English armies under William (supplemented by European mercenaries) and the Irish armies under James (with 7,000 French reinforcements) met on the Boyne in July 1690. The decisive defeat of James secured the Protestant ascendancy for many years to come; the battle deserves its place in Protestant celebrations, for it was a crucial event. For the Catholics it implied renewed confiscations and the exile of many thousands of their gentry.

During the eighteenth century the Protestants still held their memories of insecurity, and by the resolute enforcement of penal laws they attempted to hamper and degrade the Catholic population. They did not suppress the Catholic religion as such; but, by closing all other normal outlets at home for the energies of intelligent men in the professional classes, they left the priests as the obvious source of political leadership, and in the long run strengthened the political power of the Catholic Church.

The unity of the Protestant community against the dangers of 1689 soon fell apart, and the dominant Anglican group proceeded to discriminate against the dissenters—notably the Presbyterians of Ulster. The Presbyterians were important in trade, and increasingly in industry; and they came to be resentful of the political power of the Anglican landed gentry, and of the restrictions placed by England on Irish trade. The complex political history of the later eighteenth century need not concern us here, save for one significant event. In 1791 societies of 'United Irishmen' were founded in Belfast and Dublin, whose aims were to form a 'brotherhood of affection, a communion of rights and a union of power among Irishmen of every religious persuasion, and thereby to obtain a complete reform of the legislature, founded on principles of civil, political and religious liberty'. This opened up the possibility of a union between radical Dissenters and Catholics against the 'establishment' and of bringing in the power of revolutionary France to change the political order of Ireland. In fact it led to an ineffective armed rising in 1798, which was quickly suppressed; its main consequence was that it alarmed both the Irish ruling class and the English Government, and led to the abolition, in 1800, of the Irish Parliament. But before the rising broke out the defensive reaction of many Protestants to any improvement in the status of their Catholic rivals became apparent; the Orange societies, first formed about 1795 'to maintain the laws and peace of the country and the Protestant constitution', helped the Government to maintain order.

In the nineteenth century Ireland was subject to rule by a Parliament in London, and this lent more substance to the complaints of Irish patriots about alien rule. It can hardly be claimed that England ruled Ireland well during this period; some see in her actions a continued malice against the Irish people (even to the accusation of deliberately creating, or at least tolerating, the Great Famine), but the predominant view seems to be that Parliament lacked understanding of Irish problems, and the administration was dilatory, neglectful, and over-influenced by the *laissez faire* ideas of the time. The immeasurable catastrophe of the Great Famine, which began with the failure of the potato crop in the autumn of 1845, fixed in many Irish minds an image of the Englishman as the callous evicting landlord, unmoved by the utter destitution of their race. Old animosities were hardened, even in the North, which was not so gravely affected as the rest of the country. Throughout the nineteenth century, too, thinking Irishmen could see how their country's agriculture and industry were regarded as mere appendages of the British economy. To the Irish nationalist the case for reform seemed overwhelmingly strong; and it was indeed strong enough to move the consciences of many Englishmen. The significant change during the nineteenth century was the growth of an opinion in England which favoured Home Rule (which, in a period of Catholic emancipation and extending suffrage, would mean Catholic rule) for Ireland. In the nineteenth century, such an idea could never have taken much root in a Protestant Irish Parliament; but it could be passed by the votes of a largely English Parliament. The failures of economic policy in Ireland also strengthened the hands of the Government in attacking a vital part of the Ascendancy, by seeking to extend the rights of tenants and to limit those of landlords.

To Catholics, the growing strength of Home Rule sentiment in the Liberal Party was a simple recognition of just rights, won by the agitation of Irish patriots. To the Protestants of the North it was a re-awakening of old fears; and, in areas which had a Protestant majority, it was argued that even principles of abstract justice should prevent the submission of Protestants to Catholic rule. As early as 1843 a petition was organized in Belfast for the maintenance of the Union, or, if Home Rule came, for giving Ulster a legislature of its own. The industrial development of Ulster, and certain features of her agriculture which gave the farmer greater stability, set the Province apart from the rest of the country in matters other than the balance of religions; and the interests of her industrial leaders lay with the industrial classes in England, rather than with the landed gentry of the South.

The Protestant agitation against Home Rule widened the division between the two communities; evangelical sentiment was strong, fiery speeches against papal tyranny were made, the Orange Order was strengthened, and (in 1886) communal rioting broke out in Belfast. But it was also a means by which the Conservatives, in support of the Protestant Ascendancy, could delay the progress towards Home Rule. Lord Randolph Churchill, visiting Belfast in 1886, coined the phrase 'Ulster will fight: Ulster will be right', and he had previously written: 'I have decided some time ago that if the G.O.M. (i.e. Gladstone) went for Home Rule, the Orange card would be the one to play.'

By the accidents of politics, the closing decades of the nineteenth century were a period of predominantly Conservative rule, and two brief Liberal Ministries failed to pass a Home Rule measure. The Liberal Government of 1906 did not depend on the support of Irish members, and it gave priority to other reforms; but in 1910 the Irish held the balance of power, and it was clear that Home Rule would at last be granted. To many Catholics the long delay in granting such a measure was proof of British perfidy, of her determination to hold on to Ireland, even if to do so was against all her vaunted principles of freedom and justice. In consequence, the delay led to the growth of groups which sought power by force or non-violent resistance instead of by constitutional means: the

Fenians, originating in New York in 1858, and influenced by the hatred of England among those who had fled to America during and after the Great Famine; Sinn Fein, founded by Arthur Griffith at a convention in the Rotunda at Dublin in 1905. (Of Griffith it was said that he believed that nothing would be gained by appeals to 'any such myths as English justice or English mercy'.) There was also a marked revival of interest in all things Gaelic, or having roots in the customs of the Irish race. Many distinguished people, from North as well as South, were greatly concerned to foster the Gaelic language and literature, and the movement found support from Protestants as well as Catholics. On balance, however, the interest in things Irish (and in a language unintelligible to almost all the English) strengthened the nationalist cause. There was also a growth of republican labour sentiment, mainly in the South, under the influence of James Connolly.

To the Unionists of the North, however, the delay was an opportunity to organize. By the time that the Home Rule Bill was before Parliament in 1911, they had drafted a constitution for a Provisional Government of Ulster and had raised a volunteer force to defend 'Protestant liberties'. In 1912 nearly half a million citizens subscribed to a Solemn League and Covenant, pledging themselves to use 'all means which may be found necessary to defeat the present conspiracy to set up a Home Rule Parliament in Ireland. And in the event of such a Parliament being forced upon us we further solemnly and mutually pledge ourselves to refuse to recognize its authority.' Just as the nationalist cause is supported by 'chapel gate collections', so here the link between politics and religion became apparent, for the Covenant was made available for signature in the vestibules of churches. The British Government was in a weak position to deal with the threat of all-out resistance, which had a lot of support from the Conservatives; it was uncertain if the Army would be ready to suppress a Protestant insurrection. Clandestine gun-running took place at Larne and Bangor in 1914, and the Ulster Volunteer Force was growing in strength.

Then a further delay was enforced by the First World War; and war proved to be the enemy of gradual constitutional change. At Easter 1916 there was a nationalist rising in Dublin, originally with hopes of German support; when it had been suppressed it became clear that power had passed from the moderate constitutional nationalists to Sinn Fein. In 1920 the British Parliament passed the Government of Ireland Act, which provided for two Irish Parliaments, one in the North and one in the South, and for a Council of Ireland to link them (p. 37). Such a solution was too late to operate in full; British power was dissolving in the South, terrorist activity was widespread (see p. 128), and political power lay with those who wanted a fully independent State covering the whole island. By the treaty of December 1921 Britain conceded what was virtually Dominion Status to the Irish Free State in the South, subject to the right of the North to stay out.

To Catholic and nationalist opinion, this was a temporary settlement, regarded by many as extorted by threat of immediate war; the area of Northern Ireland was bound to be abridged when the Boundary Commission got to work (for much of the counties of Fermanagh, Tyrone, Londonderry, and Armagh had a Catholic majority); the remaining State would prove unworkable, and the device of the Council of Ireland could perhaps be revived to create a central authority for the whole country. The Protestant opinion was that just demands had been conceded after a righteous battle, though many would have preferred direct rule from London to the creation of a separate Parliament with limited powers. The Protestants saw no reason why they should give up an inch of the six Ulster counties which they now controlled; many would have preferred to hold all the nine counties of the province of Ulster, for there were substantial Protestant interests in Donegal, Cavan, and Monaghan.

Faced with this opposition, the Free State delegate to the Boundary Commission eventually gave up the fight. Exactly what took place is not clear, but the nationalist case is that the Chairman of the Commission, Mr. Justice Feetham of the South African Supreme Court, was not impartial. Nevertheless, in 1925 the Free State Government agreed to accept the existing boundary in exchange for financial concessions from Britain. This has been claimed as, in effect, a *de jure* acceptance of the Northern Ireland State; but the agreement was regarded in the South as having been accepted under conditions which justified its early repudiation. It was in effect repudiated by the Constitution of 1937, which claims to relate to the whole island, and which treats the six northern counties as parts of the State temporarily not under control from Dublin.

For the whole period of the independent existence of the Irish Free State and Republic, most of its politicians have been prisoners of a public opinion which would allow no fresh approach to the problem of partition. The key to popularity has been to represent the people of the North as anxious for release from the tyranny of an occupying army, and propaganda has had little regard for the many-sidedness of truth. For the whole period, also, sporadic terrorist activity has occurred on the Border, providing an added reminder that the idea of a United Ireland is still alive. Thus the ancient fears of the Protestant community are preserved and reinforced. On the other hand forty years of relative stability have meant that some of the younger generation, both of Protestants and of Catholics, have become willing to question the traditional views of their communities, and to see some merit in the arguments of their opponents.

Few British people are proud of the whole British record in Ireland. But, as has been suggested above, there is room for considerable differences of interpretation of the historical record. How far were crucial events, such as the arrival of Henry II or the Cromwellian pacification, inevitable in the circumstances? How far is it right to try to restore a past condition of the island, at great cost to people now living who have no responsibility for the past record? It can be argued that the political unity of Ireland was achieved by British arms and British administration, and that there is nothing particularly patriotic about trying to re-establish it. On the other hand, it can be argued that the present settlement is neither just nor logical, and cannot endure. Brief as our survey necessarily is, we hope that we have sufficiently illustrated the origins of some of the strong feelings still present in the two communities in Northern Ireland.

CHAPTER 2

THE OTHER MAN'S RELIGION

It is still occasionally possible to find in the Northern Ireland press advertisements such as

> WANTED—Reliable cook-general, Protestant (Christian preferred)

This is not only an indication of the importance of religion in matters of employment (a matter further considered in Chapter 6); it is a reminder that the Protestant community is divided into many churches and sects, and that some of these would confine the name 'Christian' to those who can claim a conscious experience of a moment of salvation.

'Religion' provides a question in the Northern Ireland census, and the census returns reveal that, out of 1,370,921 persons of all ages enumerated in 1951, only 5,865 failed to state a religion, 221 claimed to be freethinkers, and a mere 64 claimed to be atheists. (The corresponding census returns for 1961, however, show 28,447 as having failed to state a religion.) In the Netherlands in 1947 no less than 17 per cent of those enumerated gave no reply to a question about their denomination.[1] The main denominations in Northern Ireland in 1951 and 1961 were:

				1951	1961
Roman Catholic	.	.	.	471,460	498,031
Presbyterian	.	.	.	410,215	413,006
Church of Ireland	.	.	.	353,245	344,584
Methodist	.	.	.	66,639	71,912
Brethren	.	.	.	17,845	n.a.
Baptist	.	.	.	11,870	n.a.
Congregationalist	.	.	.	9,346	n.a.
Non-subscribing Presbyterian (i.e. Unitarian)	.	.	.	6,273	n.a.
Reformed Presbyterian	.	.	.	3,902	n.a.
Elim Pentecostal Alliance	.	.	.	1,956	n.a.
Total Enumerated	.	.	.	1,370,921	1,425,462

[1] *Statesman's Year Book*, 1960, p. 1250.

These ten account for almost all the population, and the first three account for nearly 90 per cent. One per cent of the population is divided between about 130 other Christian denominations and non-Christian religions.

Figures of church attendance or active membership are usually difficult to interpret. A distinction must be made between those attending church on a particular Sunday, those who would claim to be 'regular attenders' but who miss one or two Sundays in a month, those who go to church on special occasions (such as Easter Sunday) but only occasionally during the rest of the year, and those who would claim to be 'active members' but are prevented from attending by age, illness, or home responsibilities. Furthermore, regular church attendance is a duty for Catholics, whereas many Protestants do not put so much stress on regularity. Consequently, Protestant church attendance figures underestimate the degree of interest in the church membership. The easiest idea to handle is, however, that of actual attendance at one or more services on a particular Sunday. Thus, for England, Rowntree and Lavers[2] record that attendances in York were 35·5 per cent of the adult population in 1901, 17·7 per cent in 1935, and 13·0 per cent in 1948; these figures overstate individual attendances, since they count a person twice if he attended church more than once on the Sundays concerned. In High Wycombe in 1947, 10·5 per cent of the adult population attended church on an average Sunday. About 30 per cent of the attendances at York, and about 20 per cent at High Wycombe, were at Catholic churches; allowing for the higher rate of attendance of Catholics (probably about 60 per cent of adult membership even in England), these figures confirm the impression that Protestant church attendance in England was about 10 per cent of the non-Catholic adult population, even ten or fifteen years ago; and it may well have fallen further since. Argyle,[3] averaging a number of surveys in Great Britain between 1947 and 1957, appears to have found an attendance figure of 14·9 per cent or less than 12 per cent for non-Catholics, corresponding figures for the United States (1949–54) being 40·6 per cent and around 30 per cent; but his statistics are exceedingly obscure.

[2] *English Life and Leisure* (Longmans, Green, 1951).
[3] M. Argyle, *Religious Behaviour* (Routledge, 1958).

In contrast, a figure of 45 per cent has been quoted for Protestant church attendance in Ireland (i.e. predominantly in Northern Ireland, since only a tenth of Irish Protestants live in the Republic).[4] Even though this would imply a much higher proportion of people who, by occasional attendance or in other ways, maintain an active interest in church affairs, we think that the figure is too low. Out of 1,340 Queen's University undergraduates questioned in November 1959,[5] 61 per cent claimed to have attended church the *previous* Sunday, or 64 per cent if atheists (numbering 9), Jews, and non-Christian overseas students are excluded. The proportions attending church by denomination were:

Roman Catholic	94%
Methodist	64%
Presbyterian	59%
Church of Ireland	46%

These figures would be consistent with an average attendance on a particular Sunday for Protestants of around 50–55 per cent. University students may be more religious than the average, though we think this unlikely; being active and without home ties, they are more able to go to church; but (on the other hand) they have a minority of women, and women are better churchgoers than men.

At least it seems fair to conclude that the church attendance percentage for Northern Ireland is probably higher than in England at the beginning of the century, and for Protestants may well be four to six times as high as the present figure for England. From our observation we would confirm that a very high proportion of Catholics have an active connexion with their church, probably well over 90 per cent. Protestants of most denominations are somewhat more lax in church attendance, which, as mentioned above, is not such an insistent duty as for Catholics. Laxity in attendance has also been encouraged among better-off people by the Sunday use of the motor-car, but a very high proportion of Protestants would likewise claim an active interest in their church.

[4] Rev. C. A. M. Meldrum, quoted in *Belfast News-Letter*, 21 March 1960.
[5] *The Gown*, 20 November 1959.

The social pressure towards conformity with a churchgoing population remains strong; and church social groups, youth organizations, sports clubs, and mission meetings are an important part of the lives of many people.

But interest in one's own church may go side by side with a considerable ignorance of the 'other man's religion'. The purpose of this chapter is to examine some of the ideas which Ulster Protestants and Catholics have about each other, and to see what relation they bear to the ascertainable facts. We do this because it is clear that the conflict between the two communities is in part revealed by the 'image' which they hold of each other on religious matters—and by whether this image is true or false.

What, first of all, do members of the two communities think of each other's spiritual condition? Our inquiries suggest that many Protestants believe that the Church of Rome teaches that salvation is to be found only in communion with her, and that in consequence they are regarded by their Catholic fellow-citizens as heretics doomed to eternal damnation. A letter in the correspondence columns of the *Belfast News-Letter* of 17 November 1960, by the Rev. Ian R. K. Paisley (the leader of a separate Protestant group), illustrates this point. The writer is answering a Catholic correspondent.

'I would also remind Dr. X. that his official creed, the creed of Pope Pius IV, Article II, states: "I likewise undoubtedly receive and profess all other things delivered, defined, and declared by the Sacred Canons and General Councils, and particularly by the Holy Council of Trent; and I condemn, reject, and anathematize all things contrary thereto, and all heresies which the Church condemned, rejected, and anathematized." As his Church has officially anathematized (cursed to hell) all Protestants I think he should be the last to talk of Christian love.'

If this represents the true position, it could hardly be regarded as conducive to friendly co-operation. The facts are a little more complicated. To the Roman Catholic Church, the Protestant is probably a heretic, but he is not by that fact alone excluded from salvation; indeed, in 1952 Father Leonard Feeney of Boston was excommunicated by the Holy See for putting forward the over-zealous belief that no one outside the Catholic Church can be saved. A fair statement of the orthodox view is, we are informed, given in the following quotations:[6]

'No man . . . who, on coming to know the true Church, refuses to join it can be saved. Neither can he be saved if, having once entered the Church, he forsakes it through heresy or schism . . . He who severs himself from the Church severs himself from Christ, and cannot be saved, for in Christ alone is salvation.'

God, however, 'will not condemn those who through inculpable ignorance are unaware of His precept, who serve Him faithfully according to their conscience, who have a sincere desire to do His will, and therefore, implicitly, the desire to become members of His Church.'

However, 'in view of the fact that the Church stands plainly before the eyes of men like a city on a mountain-top, that the words of her ministers have gone forth to the ends of the earth, we do not venture to say that such cases are typical of large numbers. We are certain, at all events, that for men deprived of the abundant graces at the disposal of those who belong to the visible membership of the Church, salvation is not easy.'

There is clearly room here for differences of interpretation. Is the Northern Ireland Protestant so much divided, by history and long custom, from his Catholic neighbours, that he must be regarded as 'inculpably ignorant' of the ways of Rome? Or has he had, in a community one-third Catholic, so many chances of seeing the Church 'like a city on a mountain-top' that he must be regarded as 'knowing the true Church' and refusing to join it? We have no doubt that a few of the more zealous, both of priests and lay people, take the latter view, and to this extent the common Protestant view of Catholic belief is justified. But we would judge the more general Catholic view to be more charitable—not condoning what they regard as 'heresy', but disposed to give the heretic the benefit of the doubt, and to suppose that he does not know any better.

Similar differences exist in Protestant views of the Catholic Church. Although perhaps only a few would use the term 'heresy' in any precise sense, there is no doubt that an overwhelming majority of Ulster Protestants regard the Church of Rome as

[6] The Most Rev. M. Sheehan, *Apologetics and Christian Doctrine* (M. H. Gill, 1955, 4th edition), Part I, pp. 135, 161.

gravely in error.[7] Some in the evangelical sects, and in congregations of the main denominations under strong evangelical
influence, believe that the beginning of salvation is marked by a
personal experience of 'coming to know the Lord Jesus Christ'
from which the Catholic, by his various errors of belief and
practice, will tend to be excluded. But again we would judge the
more general and settled Protestant view to be that Catholic error,
though no doubt a cause of grief to the Heavenly Father, is not
such as to warrant an assumption of exclusion from salvation.

Thus far, therefore, relations may be described as those of a
cold war—each side profoundly conscious of the wrongness of
the other, but neither being on the whole ready to carry condemnation to its limit. The next point arises out of the contrast between
the unity of the Catholic Church and the fragmentation of the
Protestant community into numerous denominations and sects.

In Catholic thought, this fragmentation is the natural result of
heresy; it arises because too much spiritual interpretation has been
left to the individual and not enough attention paid to the Church
whose views have developed through the inspiration of her saints
and theologians over many centuries. But there is, of course, a very
real Protestant unity in defence of the freedoms associated with
the Reformation and the Protestant Ascendancy; at moments like
the signing of the Ulster Covenant, the theological differences
between the denominations are no longer considered important.
As we have suggested in the last chapter, this Protestant unity is
a modern development, for in the eighteenth century there was
antagonism between the Church of Ireland and the Presbyterian
and other Nonconformist Churches. Bickering still continues—
for instance, over the appointment of school-teachers at village
schools—but it is now quickly forgotten in face of any threat of
'domination by Rome'.

[7] Little sympathy would be found in this divided community for an application to both Protestant and Catholic of the words of Isaac Pennington: 'Oh,
how sweet and pleasant is it to the truly spiritual eye to see several sorts of
believers, several forms of Christians in the school of Christ, every one learning
their own lesson, performing their own peculiar service, and knowing, owning
and loving one another in their several places and different performances to
their Master.' (*Works*, 3rd ed., 1784, vol. I, p. 444. From 'An Examination of
the Grounds or Causes which are said to induce the Court of Boston, in New
England, to make that Order or Law of Banishment, upon Pain of Death,
against the Quakers'.)

The fragmentation of the Protestant community tends, we suggest, to make Protestants overestimate the unity of the Church of Rome. It appears to many Protestants as a vast international empire, run on 'totalitarian' principles and instantly obeying the regulation of the Pope—a Goliath against which a little Protestant sect must defend itself with the sling of Truth. The correspondence columns of the *Belfast News-Letter* (4 November 1960) again illustrate the point. The following is a letter from the General Secretary of the Christian Fellowship Centre and Irish Emancipation Crusade:

'We desire to place on record our deep dismay and sorrow at the proposed visit to the Pope by his Grace the Archbishop of Canterbury. This is indeed a grievous blow to our evangelical position, and a step which will inevitably draw the judgment of God on Church and State. We would call upon Christian people in all our Churches to devote themselves increasingly to prayer. We need delude ourselves no longer. The die is cast—the step has been taken. The most we can do now is to pray for courage and faith, that we might be true to the simplicity of the gospel in this dark hour and in the darker days that lie before us.

'We respectfully suggest that in those Churches and Mission Halls where evangelical truth is still cherished, the national anthem should be sung as a prayer next Sunday, with the congregation and minister kneeling in the attitude of prayer.'

It takes, however, only a slight acquaintance with Catholicism in other countries to recognize that there is within that Church considerable diversity, and that many subtle differences of approach can be shown even by those who accept the definition of dogma in the same words. The Roman Catholic Church in Ireland reflects the long history of oppression and persecution, especially during the days of the penal laws; it is paternalistic, giving the parish priest the influence and reverence which naturally belongs to an educated man serving a poor community. It is also markedly 'puritan', setting up many barriers against real or assumed moral dangers; we are told that in consequence it sometimes appears to Catholic visitors from overseas to be narrow-minded, concerned with the minutiae of regulation and censorship rather than with great principles. It is probable that the conflict of Protestants and Catholics causes elements in both groups to hold extreme and narrow-minded views.

We find no evidence in Catholic circles of any fear of substantial conversions to Protestant belief (provided the two communities are kept apart) though there is much concern about the possible lapse from all church membership of those who emigrate to England. The Protestant denominations are more effective in their faithful defence of the Reformation than they are in extending it. In consequence, Catholic fears are concerned with the political, social, and economic dominance of Protestants, rather than with Protestant belief as such. It is almost equally true that in this sharply divided community the Protestant denominations have little reason to fear the conversion of their members.

One point is a source of concern to both communities, namely the problem of mixed marriages. In 1564 the Council of Trent, in its decree *Ne Temere*, endeavoured to make provisions against the 'rash celebration of clandestine marriages' by requiring the presence of the parish priest to render them valid in the eyes of the Church. In some countries, for instance in Holland in 1741 and in Ireland in 1785, concessions were made whereby marriages outside the Church of Rome, though considered sinful, were recognized. This concession was withdrawn in Ireland in 1908; and the present position is that the parties to a mixed marriage must be married in a Catholic Church, and must both sign a declaration in four points:

1. There shall be no interference with the religion of the the Catholic party or his (or her) practice of it.
2. The Catholic party shall endeavour in every reasonable way to bring the non-Catholic party to the faith.
3. All the children of the marriage shall be baptized and brought up in the Catholic faith.
4. The parties shall not present themselves either before or after the Catholic marriage before a non-Catholic minister of religion for any religious ceremony.

The third requirement implies, of course, that the children must go to Catholic Schools; by this means the effectiveness of the Church's influence can be ensured.

So definite an assertion of dominance in mixed marriages is naturally a source of great Protestant resentment. We find that some Protestants believe that the Roman Catholic Church encourages mixed marriages because it will thereby gain control of the children, and thus support the population trends which are (as we shall see later, p. 107) a source of weakness to the Protestant position. But the facts seem to be that all churches in Ulster strongly discourage mixed Protestant–Catholic marriages; and in doing so they are wise, for the tensions existing in a mixed marriage frequently disrupt family life, and are an important source of social problems.

Mixed marriages cannot, of course, be wholly prevented, for there are many influences in popular culture which glorify 'love at first sight'. But the segregation of the two communities, in education and social life, is so complete that the probability of finding that the loved one 'digs with the wrong foot' is much reduced. We have not been able to obtain any statistics on mixed marriages, but we would judge that they remain relatively very few; the matter attracts attention as a point of principle rather than because of its widespread practical importance.

Just as Catholic fears are centred on the attributes of an existing Protestant Ascendancy, so Protestant fears are centred on a judgement of what would happen if there were ever to be a Catholic Ascendancy. This judgement is largely formed by looking at what has happened south of the Border. It must first be realized that there is inevitably a difficulty, in any Christian country, in defining the relative functions of Church and State; but most people would probably agree that the Church has a right to put forward its views on matters of secular policy which have a moral implication, and that the views of a church or churches commanding the allegiance of a majority of the population must inevitably carry great weight. On these grounds, it would seem perfectly natural to a Presbyterian in the North that the Government should follow the views of his General Assembly about the Sunday opening of bars, just as it seems natural to a Catholic in the South that the Government of the Republic should follow the views of the hierarchy about divorce, the censorship of publications, or the sale of contraceptives. What the Protestant fears, therefore, is in part the natural effects which would follow if he were to find himself in a minority.

It is a general Protestant belief, however, that the 'interference' of the Church of Rome in politics goes beyond the right functions of a church, and is a grave threat to civil and religious liberty. This belief is founded on certain particular and well-known examples, and on a more general assertion about clerical interference in politics. We will take some of the particular examples first.

In 1950 Dr. Noel Browne, Minister of Health in a Coalition Government of the Republic under Mr. Costello, introduced a scheme generally known as the 'Mother and Child Bill' which amongst other things proposed free maternity care and education in child-bearing. Apparently the Irish Catholic hierarchy had objected previously (in 1947) to a somewhat similar scheme, proposed by Mr. de Valera's Government; though Dr. Browne was not aware of this, and believed that there was nothing contrary to his Church's teaching in his own scheme. But the hierarchy, after a meeting at Maynooth College, wrote on 10 October to the Taoiseach (Prime Minister) informing him that the Bill would be unacceptable on two main counts, firstly that the State had no competence to give instruction on questions dealing with sex relations, chastity, and marriage, and secondly that they did not agree with the extension of State medical service. The Cabinet called on Dr. Browne to withdraw his Bill; this he refused to do and he had to resign from office.

On 7 April 1960 three men (two of them priests) were accused of assaulting a member of the Jehovah's Witnesses engaged in colportage in the town of Wexford. The local parish priest had warned the Jehovah's Witness not to bother Catholics with his literature; when he persisted there was a skirmish in the street. The District Justice found evidence of a 'technical assault', and in applying the Probation Act to the three defendants said of the Jehovah's Witnesses: 'I regard them as engaged in a calculated and dangerous conspiracy against the peace of the country, and that peace I must help to preserve.' In an earlier case at Killaloe (1958) the Justice did not find in favour of some colporteurs who alleged assault, and said that they were disturbers of the peace in giving out literature containing statements contrary to the belief of the majority. On such incidents, many Protestants would base a belief that the independence of the judiciary in Catholic countries is not to be trusted.

It is also noted that, although the hierarchy has condemned in strong terms the activities of those who disturb the peace of the Border by armed force, this condemnation does not appear to be effective, and considerable demonstrations of popular goodwill for the resistance forces have occasionally occurred in the South— some with the apparent approval of the priests. Protestants are disposed to argue from this that the Bishops are taking a hypocritical attitude, at once condemning and condoning the use of force against Northern Ireland. It is possible, however, that the general Protestant view overestimates the power of the Bishops over their people in temporal matters.

Looking farther afield, much stress is laid on the persecution of Protestants in Spain and in Colombia. It is generally admitted that the Protestant Churches are well treated in the Republic; but the suspicion remains that the basic intention of the Church of Rome is to destroy by its intolerance the civil and religious liberties won in past centuries. Thus in 1950 the General Assembly of the Presbyterian Church in Ireland 'received' (i.e. accepted in principle) a report on the duties of a Christian in relation to political and religious differences in Ireland, which contains these words:[8]

'When a Protestant is intolerant he is false to his principles, and we regret to say that there have been such cases; but for a Roman Catholic intolerance is in considerable measure an accepted principle. . . .

'One root of the Catholic/Protestant conflict, especially here where numbers are sometimes nearly equal, is the fact that the Roman Catholic Church is a world-wide religious organisation that seeks to gain control of the institutions of mankind and of public life generally; it is not merely a Church, it is a political organisation. And as long as it maintains this position, we are inevitably confronted by irreconcilable factors, which no desire to compromise or placate can make agree. Thus the Protestant often fears the dangers of the violation of his freedom and/or ecclesiastical power in religious, political and social affairs.'

Such fears can certainly be supported from Roman Catholic literature. Thus Dr. Sheehan writes:[9]

'The Church, commissioned by Christ to preach the Gospel, and clothed with infallibility, can never be unwilling to suppress erroneous

[8] *Report of the General Assembly*, 1950, pp. 88, 90.
[9] Op. cit., p. 197.

doctrine. The Church and every lover of truth must necessarily be intolerant of error. The so-called tolerance of the present age is not tolerance in the strict sense. It is due either to the incapacity to persecute, or to utter indifferentism in religious matters.'

Monsignor Knox thought that, where there was an overwhelming majority of Roman Catholics, it might be necessary 'even to deport or imprison those who unsettled the minds of its subjects with new doctrines'.[10]

Father Cavalli, a Jesuit, writes:[11]

' . . . In a State where the majority of the people are Catholic, the Church asks that error shall not be accorded a legal existence, and that if religious minorities exist they shall have a *de facto* existence only, not the opportunity of spreading their beliefs.'

But these views, taken from their context, probably give a false impression of the complexities of Catholic teaching on the relations of Church and State. It is true that the Catholic Church desires to work in harmony with the State; but this harmony should imply that each will keep to its own business, the Church to its task of saving souls, the State to its duties of temporal control. The State will operate within the framework of divine laws; but these laws impose an absolute respect for freedom of conscience, and it is no part of the State's duty to obstruct non-Catholic religions or to compel any man to enter the Catholic Church. It will interfere with the right of a human being to live according to the truth as he knows it only if this is necessary for the preservation of public order or the protection of morality.

There is nothing in such liberal Catholic teaching to which Protestants can object; but many would reply that the practice of Catholicism is different from its principles. It is, for instance, said that in Northern Ireland priests interfere directly in politics, generally in support of nationalist candidates, thus being (from the point of view of the Unionist) engaged in treason against Her Majesty the Queen. It is, of course, true that the Irish priesthood is predominantly 'nationalist' (i.e. believing in the unity of all Ireland as a single, predominantly Catholic, State): it has been

[10] *The Belief of Catholics* (Benn, 1927), pp. 241–2.
[11] *La Civiltà Cattolica*, 3 April 1948, translated in J. S. Whale, *The Protestant Tradition* (Cambridge University Press, 1955), pp. 238–9.

suggested to us that the influence of Maynooth is strong in support of such an attitude. But it is strongly denied by Catholics that the priests use their influence to instruct people how to vote. The evidence on the matter is inconclusive. It seems certain that Catholic votes have on occasions been cast in unexpected directions —e.g. for a Unionist, to keep a more anti-Catholic Independent Unionist out (see p. 48); but this might simply be intelligent choice by the electors, influenced by lay Catholics, rather than Church intervention. We have been told of particular priests alleged to be active in organizing the vote, and of particular voters who have said that they were 'required by the Church' to vote in a particular way. But we doubt if there is sufficient evidence of any general Church action to organize the Catholic vote in the Province; the more likely explanation is that the Catholic community is so closely knit in social and political matters that it happens naturally that those who worship together also vote for the same candidate. In some country districts, the priest is often called on (as an educated man who is above local jealousies) to chair meetings, and his presence at political gatherings may arise from this custom.

There are also Catholic complaints of Protestant clerical interference in politics. These arise because the Orange Order (see p. 46 below) has both religious and political aspects. It is organized in lodges with a chaplain, and these lodges are sometimes based on the congregation of a particular church. It is plain for any man to see that on 12 July, in the parades of the Orange Lodges, many ministers walk at the head of their flock, and thus show their support for a body which is certainly an influence in Ulster politics. On Orange platforms, ministers and clergy can be heard mingling the religious and the political appeal.

'It was for them to guard with increasing vigilance and prudence the priceless heritage of civil and religious liberties won for them by their forefathers, and to hand it down unsullied and unimpaired to those who came after them. If they were to achieve that goal then there must be no division in their ranks. If they allowed petty quarrels to creep in then the solidarity of their great Order would be undermined.
'Canon Uprichard went on to say that recently they had seen some attempts by some who claimed to be loyalists to disparage Lord Brookeborough and the Northern Government. It was apparent to all

that those who made the attacks were not acting in the best interests of Ulster . . . These attempts had failed and the true loyalists of Ulster had the utmost confidence in Lord Brookeborough and his Government.'[12]

Some laymen feel it part and parcel of their religious duty as Protestants to join the Order, and regard attendances at lodge meetings on a par with church attendance, but we doubt if the religious side of the Orange Order is as significant as its political aspect. Church of Ireland, Presbyterian, and Methodist ministers have told us that they support the Order because it is a way of reaching ordinary members of their congregations, because it keeps the young men steady and sober and away from harmful pursuits, or because they want to help to maintain the high ideals of the movement; we have also met ministers who have refused to help the Orange Order because they regard it as a divisive influence.

These various causes of fear and dislike come together in an impression of the 'other man's religion' which is hard to catch in words, but nevertheless influential, like an ill-informed impression of a distant country. We would judge that many Catholics rejoice in the inclusiveness and certainty of their religion, its long traditions and world-wide influence, and feel in a very direct sense members of a loving family. Their faith seems to them warm and positive, full of colour and happiness and laughter as well as of serious purpose; in contrast, they feel or imagine the Protestant churches to be cold, dour, divided and more concerned with prohibitions than with positive love. Many Protestants, on the other hand, while feeling the warmth of fellowship just as much as their Catholic neighbours, are proud to be free and adult men, finding truth in the Word of God or in the direct movings of His Spirit, and not accepting the security of the orders of a human intermediary. They believe their Catholic neighbours to be over-concerned with ritual and form, and caught up in the worship of the saints rather than of God Himself. The growth of the

[12] Canon L. V. Uprichard, reported in *Belfast News-Letter*, 13 July 1956. It should be noted that an Orangeman, while exhorted to resist the ascendancy of the Church of Rome, is advised to abstain 'from all uncharitable words, actions, or sentiments, towards his Roman Catholic brethren': see Bro. the Rev. M. W. Dewar, *Why Orangeism* (T. H. Jordan (Belfast), 1958), p. 23.

veneration accorded to Mary the Mother of Jesus is an example of a development which arouses Protestant suspicions.

The seriousness of Protestant purpose comes into collision with the habits of the Catholic community on the issue of the use of Sunday. The Catholic, having attended Mass, feels free to enjoy himself, and in fact much Catholic sporting and social activity takes place on Sunday; but there is a very strong sentiment in all Protestant denominations in favour of keeping Sunday for religious observance and avoiding secular amusements and recreations. The man who digs his garden on a Sunday earns the disapproval of his neighbours; and, symbolically, the swings in the Belfast parks are locked up. In a Catholic area, the feelings of Protestants are aroused by seeing (for instance) cinemas open on Sunday; while in a Protestant area Catholics may feel themselves unjustly limited in their reasonable activities.

Thus in Portadown, the Borough Council (Unionist) decided in 1958 to withhold a '7-day licence' from three Catholic Church Halls (to prevent the holding of Sunday dances). The Catholic bodies concerned appealed to the County Court, which in two cases upheld their appeal on the grounds that religious convictions alone did not constitute a valid reason for the withholding of a licence for seven days when such a licence would have been granted for six. Towards the end of 1959 a petition was organized by some Protestants against the 'commercialization of Sunday'; it was signed by 4,103 adult citizens and presented to the Borough Council together with a letter from the Council of the Clergy. The Borough Council decided this time to allow a 7-day licence subject to the exclusion of Sunday dancing. In March 1960 an appeal against this decision was again upheld by the County Court.

There has also been much controversy about the playing of World Cup football matches on Sunday, and at one stage the Irish Football Association decided that its sides would not play on Sundays. This decision was later reversed, but controversy continues. There is much less Protestant feeling against working overtime on Sunday; this distinction arises, we think, from an attitude of reverence towards honest labour, which is considered to have a spiritual value in itself.

If Catholics feel aggrieved at Protestant regulations there is equal feeling the other way. Many Protestants feel that it is discourteous that Catholics should refuse to join in some simple form of worship, for instance, on the occasion of a funeral. They appear to be regarding the letter of their Church's regulations as being more important than the reality of their respect for the dead.

It is unfortunate that, in addition to the substantial occasions for fearing or disliking or regarding with contempt the other man's religion and its effects, there are minor irritants which keep antagonisms alive. One is the habit of writing slogans; this is sometimes little more than a custom which amuses juveniles, but it can also be an expression of strong feelings. Sentiments such as 'Join the I.R.A.—Expel the British Forces—Stop the atrocities' are hardly likely to be found amusing by those who have suffered I.R.A. attacks; and Protestants make things worse by attacks on the Pope. 'No Pope here' is a frequent sentiment to be written on walls and roads, but the strange mixture of religious fervour and scurrility is perhaps better illustrated by this sentiment from the wall of a Belfast public lavatory: 'The fear of the Lord is the beginning of wisdom. B— the Pope.'

The attitudes of suspicion and fear which we have described tend to affect the habits of mind of the churches, in a way which further emphasizes the division. Thus many Protestants are suspicious of accretions of ritual in their services, for ritual is identified with popery; and the Church of Rome is encouraged to be more definite and rigid in its practice in Ireland, by the opposition which it constantly receives and by its fear of 'tolerance'. But there are, of course, some (especially among Protestants) who seek occasions of contact between the churches, and who desire to minimize the lesser causes of division, even though they may still recognize the importance of the greater ones. Thus there has been some co-operation in discussing the problems of Christianity in industry.

What is still, at the time of writing, uncertain is the extent to which the change of emphasis in the Catholic attitude to 'separated brethren', as shown in recent papal pronouncements, will have an effect in the special circumstances of Ireland. A new chance of co-operation and fellowship, which would lessen fear and suspicion, certainly exists; many Protestants wait with hope for small signs of an unfreezing of Catholic attitudes.

CHAPTER 3

GOVERNMENT AND POLITICS
IN A DIVIDED LAND

THE political background to the facts which we set out in the later chapters is essentially very simple. One great issue has so far dominated all others in Northern Ireland politics, the issue of whether or not the State should exist at all. The familiar classification of parties into Right and Left has only a subsidiary importance in Ulster. The division is between those who support the constitution and those who wish to change it; and, to the loyal supporters of the constitution, the second group is not Her Majesty's Opposition, an alternative government, but a gathering of those who are intent on treason against Her Majesty by robbing her of part of her rightful dominions. Such language may sound old-fashioned, but the sentiments which give rise to it still keep their vigour.

Equally, to those who wish to change the constitution, the ruling majority is not regarded as a valid expression of the people's will, but as the relic of a foreign tyranny, maintained by the threat of armed force. Bernard Shaw summed up this 'nationalist' attitude in the preface to *John Bull's Other Island*:

'A healthy nation is as unconscious of its nationality as a healthy man is of his bones. But if you break a nation's nationality it will think of nothing else but getting it set again. It will listen to no reformer, to no philosopher and no preacher, until the demand of the Nationalist is granted. It will attend to no business, however vital, except the business of unification and liberation.'

Yet the supporters of the constitution, though mostly called 'unionists', are also 'nationalists'—British nationalists—and they see no ground for a unification with the South which would break the unity with Britain which the majority desire. It is true that, when it first came about, partition was a solution almost as unwelcome in Northern Ireland as in the South, but this was because the unionists still hoped to maintain the supremacy of the British and Protestant stock throughout Ireland. There is no doubt that now the majority in Northern Ireland would greatly prefer the indefinite continuance of partition to any reunification of Ireland which broke the link with Britain.

There is no abstract principle of political justice which makes it possible to say that one side in this divided land is 'right' and the other 'wrong'; and indeed the arguments of both sides (when they attempt to rationalize their beliefs) are notably weak. There is no reason to think that an island surrounded by water should be under one political rule, and therefore nationalist references to the will of 'the majority of the people of Ireland' are of no help. Equally, there is no reason to think that the six counties, part of the old province of Ulster, enclosed by historical accident within the borders of Northern Ireland, are a natural political unit for all time, and therefore references to the will of 'the majority of the people of Northern Ireland' do not settle any question of principle. The people of Ireland, like those of Britain, have their origin in successive waves of invasion from overseas, and there is no ground for regarding the descendants of the 'invaders' of three hundred years ago as interlopers, any more than any other part of the population. Nothing of principle is settled by the use of the emotive word 'treason', for as the winds of change blow through the rest of the world, it is evident that countries often alter their ultimate allegiance. The essential issue in Ulster politics, in fact, is not amenable to discussions of principle; it is concerned with the immediate realities of political power.

The division between those who support and those who attack the constitution corresponds broadly to the division between Protestants and Catholics. We find that there are a very few Protestant nationalists who would welcome Irish unity on the terms which the Republic at present offers. There are probably more Protestants who would at least tolerate unity with the Republic if some British connexion could also be maintained— for instance, if there were a wider federation of Europe, or if the Republic became a member of the Commonwealth. There is a significant minority of educated Catholics who feel a loyalty to Britain or to Northern Ireland, and who have no desire to upset the present constitution. It is sometimes asserted that Catholic citizens in general would hesitate to cast their votes for nationalism in a secret ballot if they really thought that union with the South would occur—for they would be afraid of losing the economic benefits of the British connexion. We see no way of testing such an assertion, and we cannot know if it would be true at a moment which would necessarily be one of great political excitement; but some evidence of voters 'crossing the line' appears on page 48.

The constitution and area of government, which are thus the subject of dispute between majorities of the Protestant and Catholic communities, have their origin in the Government of Ireland Act, 1920, and in Article XII of the 'Treaty' of December 1921 which created the Irish Free State. The Government of Ireland Act was an attempt at Home Rule for Ireland, which belatedly recognized the growing conflict between North and South by providing separate local Parliaments in Dublin and Belfast. But the Act, while recognizing the conflict, in effect deplored it; for it provided also for the establishment of a Council of Ireland,

'with a view to the eventual establishment of a Parliament for the whole of Ireland, and to bringing about harmonious action between the parliaments and governments of Southern Ireland and Northern Ireland, and to the promotion of mutual intercourse and uniformity in relation to matters affecting the whole of Ireland, and to providing for the administration of services which the two parliaments mutually agree should be administered uniformly throughout the whole of Ireland . . .' (10 and 11 Geo. V, Ch. 67, s. 2 (1)).

Section 3 provided that the two Parliaments might by Acts (agreed to by an absolute majority of members of the House of Commons of each Parliament at the third reading) establish a single Parliament for Ireland, to which the powers of the Council of Ireland should be transferred; and that eventually the two regional Parliaments might cease to exist.

Section 4 of the Act reserved to the Parliament of the United Kingdom (usually known in Ulster, with antique dignity, as the Imperial Parliament) certain matters, including defence, foreign affairs, foreign trade, navigation, postal services, air services, and coinage. Northern Ireland has continued to be represented in the

Imperial Parliament, though with constituencies containing larger numbers of voters than the average for constituencies in Great Britain. Section 5 prohibited all endowment of religion or discrimination against a religion in any law. Section 21 reserved all the principal taxes on income and expenditure to the Imperial Parliament, while section 23 contemplated a compulsory 'Irish contribution to Imperial expenditure', the 'Imperial Contribution'. Very little economic power was thus to be left to the regional Parliaments, though the 'burden' of the Imperial Contribution has in practice been greatly reduced by a process of skilled interpretation of the Act.

The Government of Ireland Act remains the source of authority of the Parliament of Northern Ireland; but its provisions in relation to the rest of the country could not be applied, and the proposals for the Council of Ireland and for the eventual reunification of the country therefore became of no effect. Article XII of the 1921 'Treaty' reads:

'If before the expiration of the said month, an address is presented to His Majesty by both Houses of the Parliament of Northern Ireland to that effect, the powers of the Parliament and Government of the Irish Free State shall no longer extend to Northern Ireland, and the provisions of the Government of Ireland Act, 1920 (including those relating to the Council of Ireland) shall, so far as they relate to Northern Ireland, continue to be of full force and effect, and this instrument shall have effect subject to the necessary modifications.

'Provided that if such an address is so presented a Commission consisting of three persons, one to be appointed by the Government of the Irish Free State, one to be appointed by the Government of Northern Ireland and one who shall be Chairman to be appointed by the British Government, shall determine in accordance with the wishes of the inhabitants, so far as may be compatible with economic and geographic conditions, the boundaries between Northern Ireland and the rest of Ireland, and for the purposes of the Government of Ireland Act, 1920, and of this instrument, the boundary of Northern Ireland shall be such as may be determined by such Commission.'

As mentioned on page 17, the provisions for the Boundary Commission broke down, and the Northern Ireland Government has therefore found itself exercising the powers conferred by the Government of Ireland Act within the original six counties of its area. Both the nature and the importance of the 'economic and geographic conditions' were subject to great uncertainty, and it may be, therefore, that any solution reached by the Boundary Commission would have caused as much trouble as the situation created by its failure. But it is interesting to note that when in 1921 Sir James Craig (Prime Minister of Northern Ireland, later Lord Craigavon) argued that the six counties might be given Dominion Status (thus losing their representation at Westminster), Lloyd George is said to have turned down the proposal on the grounds that it 'would stereotype a frontier based neither upon natural features nor broad geographical considerations by giving it the character of an international boundary'.[1]

The powers of the Northern Ireland Government have been generously interpreted, so that in practice the Imperial Parliament does not legislate on matters within the competence of the Northern Ireland Parliament, while in borderline cases the Northern Ireland Parliament has been enabled to legislate on matters which belong to Westminster. The constitutional machinery is as follows. There is a Queen's representative, the Governor, appointed for six years, and a legislature comprising a House of Commons of fifty-two members (elected by universal franchise) and a Senate of twenty-six members. Two members sit in the Senate *ex officio* (the Lord Mayor of Belfast and the Mayor of Londonderry), and twenty-four are elected by the House of Commons, by proportional representation, for a term of eight years. (Half the Senate retires every four years.) The Senate continues even if the Lower House is dissolved.

The franchise for the twelve members sent to the Imperial Parliament is identical with that in Britain, and the constituency boundaries are reviewed by the United Kingdom Boundary Commission. The franchise for the Northern Ireland Parliament is similar to that for the Imperial Parliament, with the following additions:

(a) a business premises vote, based on occupation of business premises in the constituency to the value of £10 per annum or over. (A man with premises in several constituencies can

---

[1] N. Mansergh, *The Government of Northern Ireland* (Allen and Unwin, 1936), pp. 118–19.

claim the business premises vote in one only, according to his choice.)

(b) A graduate vote for the four University seats for the Queen's University of Belfast.

These additions are, of course, survivals of plural voting which formerly existed in Great Britain also. Since (as we shall see, p. 54) Catholics are under-represented in the social groups from which the business community is drawn, the business premises vote presumably favours the Unionists as the dominant Protestant party. The University vote is by proportional representation, and one Catholic is usually returned; it is doubtful if this vote has any significant effect on the balance of the representation of the two communities in the House of Commons.

Originally the Northern Ireland House of Commons was all elected by proportional representation, with the single transferable vote, on the method defined in the Representation of the People Act, 1918. The Government of Ireland Act (s.14) allowed this system to be changed after three years, and proportional representation was in fact abolished in 1929, except for the University seats. The arguments used by the Unionist majority in favour of abolition were:

(a) that election by simple majority gives a more stable government (i.e. favours the majority party);

(b) that the constituencies were too large, and the responsibility of a member to his constituents was therefore weakened;

(c) that the system was complicated and expensive to administer, and might lead to confusion in the minds of electors.

Proportional Representation, said Lord Craigavon,

'submerges and clouds the issue. At Election times, the people do not really understand what danger may result if they make a mistake when it comes to third, fourth, fifth or sixth preferences. By an actual mistake, they might wake up to find Northern Ireland in the perilous position of being submerged in a Dublin Parliament. What I hold is, if the Ulster people are ever going—and I pray they may not—into a Dublin Parliament, they should understand that they are voting a Dublin Parliament, and not be led by any trick of a complicated electoral system, such as Proportional Representation.'[2]

[2] St. John Ervine, *Craigavon : Ulsterman* (Allen and Unwin, 1949), pp. 516–17.

In view of these arguments it is not surprising that the change was opposed by Nationalist and other non-Unionist opinion. In fact, however, it made very little difference, as these figures show:

Composition of the Northern Ireland House of Commons

	For Partition				Against Partition		Totals	
Election date	Unionist	Independent Unionist	Labour*	Farmer	Nationalist	Republican (Sinn Fein)	For Partition	Against Partition
1921	40	—	—	—	6	6	40	12
1925	33	3	3	1	10	2	40	12
1929	37	3	1	—	10	1	41	11
1933	36	3	2	—	9	2	41	11

* Here classified as 'for partition': see below, p. 49.

Recent elections do not support the view that the simple majority system leads to the *extinction* of the small party. Seven parties were represented in the 1945 House, together with two Independent members; seven parties were represented after the 1953 Election, and six after the 1958 Election, each House containing also one Independent (Catholic) member. Many members are, of course, returned unopposed, but the votes in the contested seats could be used to support the view that it is the Northern Ireland Labour Party (in 1953) and the Independent Unionists who have been under-represented, rather than the Nationalists:

1953

	Votes	Members Returned*
Nationalist	35,758	4
Northern Ireland Labour	31,063	0
Independent Unionist	26,227	1

1958

Nationalist	36,013	5
Northern Ireland Labour	37,748	4
Independent Unionist	16,037	0

* Contested elections only.

The anti-partition parties complain that it is 'undemocratic' that so many seats should be filled without a contest (twenty-five in 1953, twenty-seven in 1958). Thus the *Irish Press* commented on 14 October 1953:

'It is because of the way in which the electoral divisions have been
turned into strait-jackets that so many seats are not contested. The
1929 gerrymander so corralled the Nationalists and Unionists that it is
no longer of any value to fight . . . Britain would not dare to call itself
a democratic state if 300 M.P.s were elected without a vote being
cast . . .'

Our inquiries do not, however, support the view that 'gerrymandering' has any large influence on parliamentary (as opposed
to local) elections. A manipulation of electoral boundaries in
favour of the Unionists would be expected to have one or both
of these effects:

(a) Larger populations in Nationalist-held constituencies: in
    fact, they are on the average smaller.
(b) Small Unionist majorities in some areas, and large National-
    ist majorities in adjoining areas. Thus, if, in an area of
    four constituencies, there are out of every 100 electors
    40 Unionist and 60 Nationalist, the policy named after
    Governor Elbridge Gerry of Massachusetts would seek
    to draw boundaries with the following result:

I	13 U	12 N
II	13 U	12 N
III	13 U	12 N
IV	1 U	24 N
	40	60

There would be three areas with small Unionist majorities,
and one with a very large Nationalist majority. There is something
of this kind in Co. Fermanagh, but it seems to be an accident of
geography rather than a deliberate manipulation. In Co. Tyrone
the Nationalist majorities are very small (in 1958, 236 on an
89 per cent poll, and 937 on an 84 per cent poll). The Nationalist
concentration in the South Ward of the City of Londonderry is
assigned to the Foyle division, with a large Nationalist majority,
while the City division stretches out into the County area; but
the effect of this is that in Londonderry City and County together
the Unionists get three out of five seats, and since they claim a
bare majority of the population this result might be achieved
under any fair electoral system.

The complaints of gerrymandering, in fact, appear to be

transferred to the parliamentary from the local government field, where they properly belong (we discuss them on p. 120). It may be worth noting in passing that the assertion of some anti-partitionists[3] that they have a majority in four of the six counties taken together is not necessarily valid. In the last two elections for the Westminster Parliament (which provide the best available test, since all seats were contested) the Unionists received *votes* which were very close to an absolute majority of the total *electorate* in the four counties referred to (Armagh, Fermanagh, Tyrone, and Londonderry). This result was affected by the unpopularity of the Sinn Fein Party, which was associated with violence on the Border. The most likely interpretation, however, is that, in the 1959 Election at least, a few Catholics voted Unionist; and this weakens the validity of forecasts of electoral behaviour based on counting the adherents of different religions.

Our general conclusion is that in its composition the Northern Ireland Parliament reflects the views of the people with no more distortion than is normally to be found in democratic parliaments. Its real peculiarity is that, being elected mainly on the constitutional issue, it has no alternation of parties in office.

We will now briefly describe some of the features of the main political parties. The ruling Unionist Party has members at Westminster who accept the Conservative whip; this is the natural result of the Ulster objection to the Liberal efforts to introduce Home Rule, half a century and more ago. But within the Province the Unionists are more diverse in their interests than might be expected of a conservative party. They are above all a party of the Protestant people, and this means that they must represent both the traditional radical and independent spirit of Presbyterianism (so far as it survives) and the Anglican conservatism of landed gentry, while not forgetting the hopes and fears of a large urban working class belonging to many Protestant sects. It is true that an individual picks a political party because of his agreement with that party in the matters which he conceives to be really important; and to those Protestants for whom the constitutional issue is the only political issue of any interest, it hardly matters what the Unionist Party does or thinks about

[3] E.g. D. O'Neill, *The Partition of Ireland* (M. H. Gill, 1949, 4th edition), p. 21.

such things as education, social welfare, or economic development. It is true also that the resolute performance of the task of opposing the Nationalists tends to unite the Unionist Party in a common objection to anything which Nationalists suggest. But the party remains flexible and undogmatic, on all issues save that of the constitution; for instance, it showed no great difficulty in reproducing for Northern Ireland the legislation of the 1945 Labour Parliament, where it was appropriate; and nationalization of parts of the transport industry came earlier in Northern Ireland than in Britain.

Year after year the Unionist Party takes its stand on loyalty to the Crown and opposition to the claims of the Republic of Ireland; and it is greatly assisted in maintaining public interest in these matters by the persistent claims of Southern politicians and by the outbreaks of violence on the Border associated with the Irish Republican Army and *Saor Uladh*. The constitutional issue is not some piece of past history, now meaningless to the younger voters; it is continuously kept alive. At each General Election the Unionist Party has been able to use the same arguments, as may be seen from these extracts from leading articles in the *Belfast News-Letter*:

1929
'The issue is whether a Unionist Government shall continue to control affairs, safeguard the interest, and help to shape the destination of Northern Ireland, or whether the task is to be entrusted to some fortuitous combination of Nationalists, Socialists, and Independents.'

1933
'The issue at stake in this contest must be apparent to all. Do the Ulster people still value their birthright? Are they still insistent on retaining their full partnership with the rest of the United Kingdom within the Empire? In neither case is the issue in doubt. There remains the question which tomorrow must settle: Is the Government that for 12 years has stood, and continues to stand, for the conservation of that birthright to receive a mandate not less emphatic than before . . . The electorate must not be deceived by those who are not Unionist Party members or supporters . . . we have been warning Loyalists not to be deceived by quasi-Unionists calling themselves "Independent". Every such vote is a symptom of weakness and indecision and will be regarded as such by (Ulster's) enemies.'

1938

'Lord Craigavon's purpose in this election is to show that Ulster stands precisely where it did in relation to the Free State or rather that its people's attachment to Great Britain and the Empire is as strong as ever and that in no circumstances will they give up their place in the United Kingdom.'

1945

'From whatever angle the General Election in Northern Ireland be regarded the Constitutional question emerges as the governing issue. In Socialist quarters it was dismissed as a bogy, put forward to divert attention from realities such as economic security and the standard of living. Yet the Nationalist Party, which for a time was considering the propriety of making the Election a sort of referendum on the question by contesting each seat, has now announced that its first duty, when the results are known, will be to set up in conjunction with the people across the Border an Anti-Partition Council representative of all Ireland.'

1949

'Today Ulster people go to the poll on an issue which admits of no compromise—whether they are to continue in Union with Great Britain or to be absorbed into an Irish Republic. Never throughout the long controversy has their position been challenged more directly; at no time has the need for an unequivocal reply been more urgent.

'In Sir Basil Brooke's considered opinion, the country is in danger, its people's heritage at stake—not so much because of immediate uncertainties at Westminster as because of the Eire Government's tactics or intention. Hitherto the pressure upon Westminster has been direct; presently it is to be exerted through an international medium.'

1953

'Not the least disturbing feature of the present General Election campaign has been an increasing tendency to suggest that as Northern Ireland's position is now unassailable, the time has come when the Unionist electorate can dismiss its fears and with safety concentrate upon purely domestic issues. No more pernicious theory could be advanced; no policy is more fraught with danger.'

1958

'To throw Northern Ireland into the Republic would be fatal. It would ruin Ulster and the added weight of a ruined Ulster would sink a Republic that can only keep going as it is with the aid of emigration on a colossal scale, high tariffs, and remittances, in spite of which its unemployment problem is severe.'

1958

'While the leader of the Northern Ireland Labour Party had declared that one of its objects is to preserve and strengthen the Province's link with Great Britain, the fact remains that it is challenging candidates whose attitude towards the maintenance of the Border cannot be called into question, and has abstained from opposing men who would like to see Ulster absorbed by an all-Ireland Republic. Indeed it is being helped by Republicans. In Pottinger, for instance, the Eire Labour Party has announced that it is giving its full support to Mr. Thomas Boyd, but has warned him that if he is elected and makes "one pro-Unionist speech, or casts one pro-Unionist vote" he will be opposed at the next election.'

Thus the party keeps its constant watch and ward, seeking to discredit all other supporters of the partition of Ireland by suggesting that the constitutional issue is not safe in their hands. Behind the party, and giving it something of the character of a mass movement, stands the Orange Order—the Loyal Orange Institution of Ireland, whose numerous lodges fill the processional routes with banners and orange sashes on the Twelfth of July. The Orange Order is a mixture of the religious and the secular, the social and the political; at its best, it is an effective way of maintaining a warm and united spirit among 'Protestant brethren' from all social classes. The County Grand Lodges of the Order nominate 122 delegates to the Unionist Council out of a total of 712; but this is not a measure of their true influence, since almost all members of the Government are members of the Order, and we have received information which suggests that it would be very difficult to be accepted as a Unionist Party candidate without being a member of a Lodge.

The Unionist Party contains some members who lose no opportunity of thumping the Protestant drum, in the manner of Lord Craigavon's celebrated statement in 1937, that the Ulster Parliament was 'a Protestant Parliament for a Protestant people'. However, even this remark was intended, not as an expression of religious bigotry, but as an attack on treasonable nationalists; the religious and the political terms tend to be interchanged. There has always been a tradition in the Unionist Party in favour of justice towards Catholics, as Catholics—and, indeed, on some issues (such as grants for schools) the party can claim generosity.

The two sides of the Unionist character were illustrated by an incident in 1959. In answer to a question at a Young Unionist political school at Portstewart, Sir Clarence Graham, chairman of the standing committee of the Ulster Unionist Council, said that he did not see why a Roman Catholic should not be selected as a Unionist candidate for Parliament. He is reported to have continued: 'Will the day ever come when many of them (the Nationalists) will wish to join the Unionist Party? I do not know, but I do not rule out the possibility.' He was eloquently supported by the Attorney-General, Mr. Brian Maginess, long a leader of moderate opinion in the party. 'To shed our parochialism is not to deny our inheritance. To broaden our outlook means no weakening of our faith. Toleration is not a sign of weakness, but proof of strength. This will require some change of thinking on the part of many, and it will need on the part of some a less provocative form of speech. It will require considered words instead of clichés, reasoned arguments instead of slogans.'[4] But shortly afterwards, at Scarva, Sir George Clark, Grand Master of the Grand Orange Lodge of Ireland, stated that Roman Catholics in the Unionist Party could not be countenanced or accepted by the Orange Order.[5] The party itself unfortunately remained silent on these contending views. The Prime Minister, Lord Brookeborough, speaking at the annual dinner of the Lisbellaw branch of the Fermanagh Young Unionist Association on 20 November 1959, said:

'There is no use blinking the fact that political differences in Northern Ireland closely follow religious differences. It may not be impossible, but it certainly is not easy for any person to discard the political conceptions, the influence and impressions acquired from religious and educational instruction by those whose aims are openly declared to be an all-Ireland republic.

'The Unionist Party is dedicated to the resistance of those aims and its constitution and composition reflect that basic fact. There is no change in the fundamental character of the Unionist Party or in the loyalties it observes and preserves.

'If that is called intolerance, I say at once it is not the fault of the Unionist Party. If it is called inflexible then that shows that our principles are not elastic.'

[4] *Belfast News-Letter*, 2 November 1959.
[5] *Belfast Telegraph*, 10 November 1959.

Despite the breadth of interest within the Unionist Party, and the arguments for unity against Nationalist pressure, groups of Independent Unionists have from time to time appeared. Some, like the Progressive Unionists in 1938, have tried to stimulate the Government to more vigorous action on economic matters; others have represented an extreme or vociferous Protestant viewpoint, attacking the official Unionist Party for weakness towards the Nationalists. One of these was Mr. Norman Porter, who represented the Clifton division of Belfast in the Northern Ireland Parliament from 1953 to 1958, defeating an official Unionist candidate by 345 votes. In 1958, however, the official Unionist defeated Mr. Porter by 45 votes, again in a straight fight, and it is widely (and with some justification) believed that some of the majority were Catholic voters—an interesting case of people choosing what to them was the 'lesser of two evils'.

In recent years extreme anti-Catholic views have been revived and promoted by a body called Ulster Protestant Action. We have found it impossible to assess the extent of this body's membership and support, but its existence is a reminder of a view still important in Ulster politics. An example of its propaganda is a leaflet which purports to reproduce a 'Sinn Fein Oath', to drive 'these Protestant robbers and Brutes . . . like the swine they are into the sea, by fire, the knife, or by Poison Cup, until we of the Catholic Faith and avowed supporters of the Sinn Fein Action and Principles clear these Heretics from our Lands'.[6] The oath is plainly a fabrication. Sinn Fein is a political party, which has no oath; the Irish Republican Army has an 'affirmation' (the Catholic Church does not permit membership of an oath-bound body) which reads as follows: 'I hereby affirm that I will carry out the objects and ideals of the Irish Republican Army to the best of my ability and I will loyally obey my superior officers.'

---

[6] The vigour of the language recalls the early nineteenth-century Orange toast quoted by Arthur Bryant, *The Age of Elegance*, p. 267: 'To the glorious, pious and Immortal Memory of King William III, who saved us from Rogues and Roguery, Slaves and Slavery, Knaves and Knavery, Popes and Popery, from brass money and wooden shoes; and who ever denies this Toast may he be slammed, crammed and jammed into the muzzle of the great gun of Athlone, and the gun fired into the Pope's Belly, and the Pope into the Devil's Belly, and the Devil into Hell, and the door locked and the key in an Orangeman's pocket . . .'

Perhaps because its form of propaganda no longer carries conviction in a more tolerant community, Ulster Protestant Action does not seem to be gathering additional support; but some observers regard it as a dangerous focus for sectarian trouble if unemployment becomes more serious and prolonged.

The complications of labour politics in Ireland are very great. One line of thought descends from the great Irish socialist James Connolly, who regarded socialism and nationalism as essentially complementary. Socialist ideas about the economic and political order have never taken much root among Irish Catholics—though there is here some divergence between ideas and practice; public ownership has a large and successful place in the economy of the Republic. But a rich variety of 'Labour' candidates have at various elections sought the support of the Catholic working class of Belfast for policies which are essentially nationalism with a radical twist. Thus Mr. H. Diamond was in 1958 returned for the Falls division as 'Republican Labour', his opponent being 'Independent Eire Labour'; Mr. F. Hanna was returned for Belfast Central as 'Independent Labour'.

Another influence in labour politics, however, is the idea of a brotherhood of working men which transcends religious and political differences. Such an idea can be seen in the trade union movement, many of whose leaders favour the unity of Irish trade unions, North and South of the Border (see p. 138). This does not necessarily make them Irish nationalists, but it means that there is a body of opinion which regards economic and industrial matters as more important than the constitutional issue—just as the Church of Ireland regards the religious unity of its members, North and South, as more important than their political division.

The trouble is, however, that no Protestant working-class movement can hope for mass support for a policy which ignores the constitutional issue. The Unionist Party contains a 'labour' group, and this is a possible rallying-point for the loyalist workers of Belfast. During the war a loyalist alternative existed in the Commonwealth Labour Party, represented in Parliament by Mr. Harry Midgley; but he eventually joined the Unionist Party, and during the period 1945–50 labour politics in Ulster wholly failed to reflect the strength of the Labour Party at Westminster. Eventually, in 1949, the foundations were laid for the Northern

Ireland Labour Party in its present form, associated with the British party, and clearly on the side of those who support the constitution.[7] This party gained no seats in 1953, but in 1958 and 1962 four members were returned, probably with some Catholic as well as Protestant support.

It remains, however, uncertain how far this 'loyal opposition' can progress. It has little support outside Belfast; it is vulnerable to the standard Unionist argument about splitting the loyal vote; and there is a widespread feeling that the British Labour Party is 'not to be trusted' on the constitutional issue, and that a vote for the Northern Ireland party might in some way add to Labour's strength in Britain. It was actually the British Labour Party which (in the Ireland Act, 1949) provided the most explicit guarantee yet given of the constitution:

'It is hereby declared that Northern Ireland remains part of His Majesty's dominions and of the United Kingdom and it is hereby affirmed that in no event will Northern Ireland or any part thereof cease to be a part of His Majesty's dominions and of the United Kingdom, without the consent of the Parliament of Northern Ireland.'[8]

Nevertheless, there is some sympathy for the cause of Irish unity in the British Labour Party, which makes it difficult for an associated party to retain full Protestant support. For older but similar reasons, it has proved difficult for the Liberal Party to regain a foothold in the Province, beyond a single University seat.

Of the anti-partitionists, we have already mentioned the 'labour' groups in Catholic constituencies in Belfast. The remaining members of Parliament can be divided into two groups: those who (because they have wholly denied the validity of the Northern Ireland constitution) have refused to take their seats, preferring to work outside Parliament for the overthrow of the constitution by peaceful or violent means; and those who have taken their seats, using Parliament as a means of drawing attention to their views and to the grievances of their community. The second group is often accused by Unionists of dishonesty, since

[7] There were Labour members at Stormont from 1925 onwards, but their position on the constitutional issue was not clear. The present policy of the Northern Ireland Labour Party is set out in *Ulster Labour and the Sixties*, 1962; it includes the review of local government boundaries.

[8] 12 and 13 Geo. VI, Ch. 41, s.1 (2).

they take an oath of allegiance to a sovereign whose authority they wish to terminate.

In the 1921 Parliament, six 'Nationalists' and six of the old Sinn Fein Party were returned; all refused to take their seats. In 1925 ten Nationalists and two Sinn Feiners were elected, and this time some of the Nationalists began to attend Parliament—two in 1925, three more in 1926, and four more in 1927. In 1958 seven Nationalists, two Independents (Nationalist supporters), together with one each from Republican Labour and Independent Labour, were returned, all of whom took their seats.

The group of Nationalist M.P.s can hardly be called a party; it is a loose association of members from rural areas, whose main interest in Parliament is to maintain a protest. Their views tend to be conservative, and they are derisively called 'green Tories' by Catholics with Labour sympathies. At times the group seems to dissolve; thus in the 1955 elections for the Imperial Parliament, the Nationalists left the field to the new Sinn Fein Party, which (although apparently associated with the violent attacks on the Border) polled 132,300 votes and had two members elected. This was probably a simple transfer of the normal Nationalist vote from a party which seemed dead to the only candidates who expressed the traditional protest: it proved neither the existence of general support for the I.R.A. attacks, nor a general willingness to ignore the views of the Church. In 1959, voters were less willing to appear to support violence: Sinn Fein polled only 63,415 votes, returning no candidates.

On the whole, the anti-partition parties give the impression of being tired of the unconstructive business of carrying on a long and hopeless fight—for the balance of the communities remains much as it was forty years ago. The Anti-Partition League, once a prominent source of propaganda, seems to be no longer very active. A new body, however, was formed in 1960 called 'National Unity'. It aims at constructive opposition and co-ordination of existing Nationalist groups, with Irish unity as an ideal to be achieved only when a majority of the people of Northern Ireland desire it. We cannot judge whether this new initiative stands any chance of changing the course of Ulster politics.

CHAPTER 4

SOCIAL RELATIONS

THE divisions created by history and religion, and reflected in politics, are naturally seen also in the social structure of the Province. Several aspects of this structure are examined in greater detail in subsequent chapters; the purpose of this chapter is to give a broad picture of social structure and relations in city, town, and country, and to show how the social structure has become stable, familiar, and capable of perpetuating itself.

In order to do this, we pick out six aspects of the division between the two communities:

1. Despite intermarriage and conversion, three centuries have not obliterated the differences of national origin. In the delicate task of classifying every chance acquaintance according to 'which foot they dig with',[1] one is helped by a presumption that an Irish name will belong to a Catholic, a Scots name to a Presbyterian, and an English name to some kind of Protestant. With a little practice, one learns to avoid the pitfalls set by anglicized versions of Irish names, and by the use by both Scots and Irish of the prefix 'Mc' or 'Mac'. The 'racial' differences are still to be seen to some extent in build and facial appearance; there is a (supposedly) 'Celtic' type, which one naturally associates with membership of the Catholic Church rather than of an Orange Lodge. Of course, there has been enough mixture to make any such rules unreliable; but it is significant that they retain so much validity. We have been told of a Presbyterian minister with an Irish name, who (in connexion with a 'call' to a new church) went one Sunday to preach two test sermons. After the morning service one of the congregation said to him: 'That was a grand sermon you preached this morning, but you have a curious name and it might be no harm if you took a wee burl at the Pope the night.' We have been assured by Protestants with

---

[1] Professor Estyn Evans has suggested that this phrase for expressing a religious difference may have had its origin in regional differences in the type of turf-cutting spade used.

Irish-sounding names that this fact gives rise to a suspicion (in other Protestants) which is only gradually overcome; and English people settling in Northern Ireland are sometimes suspect, because a name which sounds Protestant to Irish ears may turn out to belong to a Catholic. In one case, this led to the almost inconceivable accident of unknowingly appointing an English Catholic teacher to a Protestant school.

2. In the towns, the two communities tend to live apart; in the country, there is much resistance to the sale of a farm to one of the other religion. In the Plantation towns, the Scots and English lived around the market or within the walls, and the Irish on the outskirts or beyond the gates. In the country (so far as it was affected by the Plantations) the Irish tended to be excluded from the good valley land and banished to the mountains. This historical segregation can be traced in the towns by the names of the streets or quarters, 'Irish Street', 'English Street', 'Scotch Street'; in the country it is more difficult to trace on the map (since Irish place-names were retained in many areas settled by English or Scots), but can often be discovered in the names borne by local people.

There are powerful reasons why segregation, once established, should continue. The Catholic chapels[2] and schools were built to serve an established Catholic community, and became a strong centre of attraction for more families of the same faith. So much social life centres on the churches that the sense of 'belonging' is difficult to maintain unless one has neighbours of the same faith. Such neighbours are more than a comfort; there is a history of faction fights in the Ulster countryside, and (up to 1935) of rioting in Belfast, and common prudence suggests that one should live with those who can be trusted to take the same side.

Where the segregation of Catholics begins to break down, this is regarded by many Protestants with alarm (however friendly they may be with individual Catholic neighbours): 'they are getting in' is the phrase one hears, and it is evident that in general

---

[2] The class-distinction between 'church' and 'chapel' now survives in Ulster, not as a difference between the edifices of the (formerly Established) Church of Ireland and the rest, but as a difference between Protestant 'churches' and Catholic 'chapels'. A Welshman settled in Ulster told us: 'When I came here, I used to say that I went to chapel, and I wondered why people crossed to the other side of the street.'

a 'mixed' area in the towns is regarded by Protestants as one which is going downhill. In consequence a Protestant landlord is unfaithful both to his own 'side' and perhaps to his long-term business interest if he sells or lets part of his property to a Catholic. In some town or country areas, sales to those of the other religion may upset the delicate balance of voting, and change the representation of the district in local government. There is naturally strong social pressure to prevent any landlord doing such a thing, though it is not always effective in withstanding economic inducements.

3. There is a marked difference in the economic status of the two communities: the Protestants tending to provide the business and professional classes, the larger farmers, and the skilled labour, and the Catholics the small farmers and the unskilled labourers. There are, of course, many exceptions to this, for instance because a Catholic business and professional class has to exist to serve the needs of the Catholic community, and this in turn creates some opportunities of skilled employment. We shall be dealing with the problem of religion in employment in more detail later (p. 93); but the broad picture is clear, and is illustrated by these figures:

Employment by Occupation (our own survey in Portadown, 1960)

	Catholic	Presbyterian	Church of Ireland	Methodist
Approximate percentage of total labour force in:				
Professional, executive, administrative occupations	1	5	6	7
Supervisory and lower managerial occupations	12	19	18	14
Skilled manual and routine non-manual work	32	50	43	58
Semi-skilled manual work	39	23	24	13
Unskilled work	16	3	9	8
	100	100	100	100

NOTE : These figures relate to 'heads of families' and others regarded as normally available for work. The classification is similar to the social class division used by the Registrar-General for England and Wales. The unemployed are assigned to their assumed normal occupation. The total number surveyed was 2,481. The Church of Ireland figures are much less reliable than the others.

Class Structure of Two Rural Areas (unpublished London University M.A. thesis by Dr. R. L. Harris)

	Catholic	Protestant
Approximate percentage of heads of families classified as:		
Upper class . .	0	18
Large farmers . .	13	20
Medium farmers .	22	30
Small farmers .	34	17
Labourers . .	22	8
Miscellaneous . .	9	7
	100	100

NOTE: These figures are based on 104 families in an area of Co. Fermanagh. 'Upper class' here means those who had adopted certain middle-class traits; 'large' farmers means that they had large farms relative to the average for the area.

It is a natural consequence of this difference in economic status that unemployment, which commonly falls with more severity on the unskilled, in Northern Ireland has a disproportionate effect on the Catholic workers. This alone does not account for the difference in the unemployment rates, since questions of job discrimination and emigration are also involved; we touch on it further in Chapter 6.

The reasons for the difference of economic status lie partly in the kind of society which was imposed by the Plantations and by the era of Protestant Ascendancy. The difference then created tends to perpetuate itself, both because of the inheritance of wealth (for instance, by a large farm remaining in a Protestant family) and because the families of unskilled workers start life underprivileged, and find it difficult to get a foot on the ladder which leads to higher economic or social status. The latter effect is probably strengthened by the greater tendency of Catholics to have large families, which (for instance) makes it more likely that a Catholic boy will have to leave school early to help augment the family income. Differences in educational provision may also have an effect (see p. 87). Whether in addition (as many Protestants suppose) there is a difference in 'national character', by which those of English or Scots ancestry tend to be thrifty, hard-working, and effective in business, and those of unmixed Irish ancestry lazy and 'shiftless', seems to us to be a matter of opinion.

4. The education of the two communities is almost wholly separate, except at university level; this is a matter further discussed on pp. 77–92. This increases the opportunity of impressing on the youth of each community the ideas of religion and of history commonly accepted in that group, and of preserving them from ever having to think about an alternative view. Thus, Protestant schools often teach mainly English history, with some Irish history as seen from the English point of view; while a Catholic school may use the study of history partly as a means of impressing on the student the story of the Irish 'national struggle for independence', and of British injustice. The Irish language is seldom studied except in Catholic schools, and we are told that knowledge of Irish culture and antiquities tends to be much greater among those with a Catholic education. Apart, however, from any divisions created by what is taught, there is a division created by the mere fact of separate education; in each community it is possible for young people to grow up, knowing many people as neighbours or as school-friends, and yet having no ties of friendship with any person of different religious persuasion. Even games depend to a large extent on religion (p. 148), and the friendly rivalry of the playing-field may not therefore do much to create ties between the two communities. The tragedy of separation is illustrated by a conversation which one of our friends overheard between his young daughter and another girl. This girl complained that, living on a new estate, she had no one to play with. 'But', she was asked, 'haven't you any neighbours to play with?' She replied, 'Yes, there are children next door, but they aren't neighbours, they're Protestants.' A similar remark could equally have been made by a Protestant about Catholic neighbours.

5. The demographic characteristics of the communities differ in the obvious way, namely that the Catholic birth rate is higher. This difference is, however, superimposed on a difference between town and country, for the countryside of Northern Ireland shares in some degree the remarkable Irish tendency to late marriage. Even in the towns, the age at marriage tends to be higher than in Great Britain; while fertility within marriage appears to be higher than in Great Britain, not only because of a higher proportion of Catholics, but also because of a higher fertility of

Protestants. Late marriage tends to reduce the birth rate, high fertility to increase it; the balance between these factors may give a different result in town and country, and therefore the birth rate for a religious group depends on the proportion of townsfolk included in it.

By itself, the higher Catholic birth rate would tend to change the social situation; but in the forty years of Northern Ireland's existence, it has been neatly offset by a higher Catholic emigration rate, so that the balance between the two communities has changed very little. Some calculations on this point appear on p. 107.

6. The social class structure of the Province is difficult to describe. It seems to us clear that in general Protestants feel superior to Catholics; this is not only a relic of the former Protestant Ascendancy over all Ireland, but also a result of the present-day fact that a Catholic is more likely to be unskilled and poor than a Protestant. Indeed, of course, the most obvious cases of poverty are to be found in Catholic families and in Catholic districts, where large families are being brought up on a labourer's wage, or on remittances from husbands who have had to emigrate to seek employment. The sense of superiority is, we think, to be found at all levels, the Protestant working class feeling itself to be more 'decent' than the Catholic, and the Protestant professional or business man feeling himself to have a more established status than his Catholic opposite number. A housewife may be heard saying, after tidying up a room, 'that's more Protestant-looking'. We find it much more difficult to assess what Catholics feel about the status of the Protestants; the assumption of superiority is clearly resented, but it is probably also in a sense accepted as one of the unpleasant facts of life.

Segregation in housing and differences in education and in employment cut so deep that many have no need to go farther than an idea of the other community 'in general', as 'they' without any personal reference. Where Protestants and Catholics are brought together as neighbours, as workmates, or in some common social activity, their relationships show sometimes a delicate desire to discern and respect differences, and sometimes a wish to emphasize them without respecting them. We see few cases of a readiness to ignore differences.

The desire to respect differences can be seen if guests arrive at a party who are not of the same religion as the other guests; word about their religious beliefs will be passed round, and everyone will be scrupulously careful to avoid embarrassing topics such as national allegiance, party politics, or religious doctrine. We have noted cases on both the Protestant and the Catholic side where a guest of the other religion was asked to come at a later time than the rest, in order that there might be time to warn the others present that they must be careful. In discussions about this survey, we have often observed that people drop their voices and look to see who is listening, and we think that this is due to a desire not to give offence rather than to a fear of controversial discussion as such. From rural areas, we hear of friendly relationships between neighbours of different religion, interrupted by a period when they see little of each other, in July and August; for these are the months when sectarian spirit is at its height, and offence is most likely to be given.

Friendly relationships thus exist with a *consciousness of difference*. The prudent keep off controversial subjects; the less prudent (or those in a more intimate degree of friendship) may indulge in friendly banter, but it will be of a kind which throughout remembers the religious difference. This is perhaps why a very large proportion of Northern Ireland jokes are about religion. 'I'll never come to Belfast again,' says a Dublin visitor, sitting down in a bus. 'It's cold and wet and full of Protestants.' 'You should take your next holiday in Hell,' comes the reply. 'It's hot and dry and full of Papishes.' There are hundreds of such jokes, by means of which one can acknowledge and pass off lightly differences which are considered too deep for serious discussion.

The desire to emphasize differences without respecting them is to be seen in the ostentatious flying of flags or chalking up of slogans; for instance, Union Jacks are flown, not only through patriotism, but sometimes to emphasize a difference from one's opponents, and papal flags are flown for the same reason. Demonstrations in areas inhabited by those of the opposite faith have a like effect.

The foregoing discussion of six aspects of division will seem to some too extreme. Of course it is true that close friendships, common cultural interests, and genuine mutual respect can and do exist between many families of opposite religion. But we have noticed that, no doubt because of an underlying desire to avoid division, people are disposed to generalize too much on the basis of individual cases of close relationship. Even where such a relationship can most easily be built, as (for instance) among the students of the Queen's University, we find that the division still cuts deep, and it remains possible for many to avoid any regular social contact with those in the opposite camp.

It is clear that the differences we have discussed react on each other, and constitute a self-perpetuating social system whose characteristics are difficult to change. Many Catholics are poor; therefore their children's opportunities in early life are limited, and the next generation also tends to be of low social and economic status. Poverty and unemployment sustain the high Catholic emigration rate, without which the social structure would alter by an increase in Catholic numbers. Segregation in education strengthens the tendency to live in separate areas. Differences in social status and in areas of residence support the religious objections to intermarriage, and therefore preserve the racial differences. It is interesting to notice how often people in both communities develop over-simple explanations to account for the observed divisions. Many Catholics believe that the only reason why they cannot get good jobs is because of a deliberate policy of discrimination directed from Stormont or (less credibly) from London. We shall have to sift what truth there is in this (see p. 93); but few seem to realize that even if there were no discrimination at all, fewer Catholics than Protestants would get good jobs because (in this generation) relatively fewer are qualified to fill them. Many Protestants believe that poverty is a natural accompaniment of Catholicism—'look at Italy and Spain'—a view which in a convenient and simple manner justifies their own economic dominance, by ignoring all other causes of Catholic poverty which lie in past history or current policy.

Let us now look at social relations in three different types of area—the countryside, the provincial town, and the city of Belfast.

1. *The Countryside*[3]

In the four 'Plantation' counties we have noted that, although the planters were permitted to have some Catholic tenants, these

[3] See Dr. R. L. Harris, 'The Selection of Leaders in Ballybeg', *Sociological Review*, July 1961, p. 137.

tended to be pushed off the fertile lowlands into the upland areas or 'mountainy districts', where the topsoil was usually thin and the land might be little better than bog. In these districts older patterns of living have to some extent survived. There is much visiting of neighbouring farms in the evenings, but mainly by the men and not their wives; in lowland areas husbands and wives visit together. People help each other at harvest time more in the poor upland farms than in the mechanized farms of the rich valleys. The 'wake' or gathering of bereaved relatives after a death is still remembered as a great social occasion and duty in the mountains.

The people of the upland areas form a closed community to a much greater extent than in the valleys, where the advent of the motor-car has done much to break down community barriers. There is little contact between the two areas, except by way of trade, and intermarriage between upland and valleys is infrequent even between those of the same faith. Intermarriage is in fact unlikely until the upland farmer has become prosperous enough to purchase a farm in the valley and enter into the higher social stratum there existing. The 'mountainy' people are suspicious of outsiders, especially inspectors and officials of all types. Educated people, such as priests, ministers, doctors, and schoolmasters, have had part of their schooling outside the district even if they were originally born there, and it is therefore hard for them to establish themselves as a real part of the community.

The sense of community is supported by a largely common religion, but it goes beyond it. Some poorer Protestants live in the upland areas, and they tend to be absorbed into the customs of the neighbourhood, working (for instance) side by side with their Catholic neighbours on the communal work of harvest. In these areas, therefore, religious differences may be insufficient to split an old and strong social structure.

In the lowland areas the picture is more complicated. We find in several parts of the Province the paradox of greater contact and neighbourly feeling between the two main religious groups than exists in the Belfast district, or even in the larger provincial towns, yet at the same time more rigidity and tension, especially in the Border areas. Where there are fewer folk and one is known over a wide area, good neighbourliness is almost enforced, for no one wants to get the name of 'a bad neighbour', or to offend against the community customs of the district. We have heard numerous stories of kindness crossing the religious borders, in ways which go beyond the exigencies of common good neighbourliness. On the other hand, whereas feelings in the Belfast area have become more tolerant of late, in rural areas (and especially those near the Border) the political and national issues have become more prominent and have not surprisingly brought a new hardness to attitudes.

Where a district depends almost entirely on the land, with little other outlet for labour except in shops, the control of farm land is an important issue. With improvements of education and the fertilizing influence of agricultural subsidies, members of the Catholic community have gradually tended to become more prosperous, and this has been shown by their entering into competition with Protestants for some of the better farms as they come up for sale. This causes anxiety amongst Protestants—that their district will become Catholic-controlled—and generally tends to 'close the ranks' and to increase segregation and bitterness. We have heard complaints from Protestants (in Fermanagh) that land purchase is organized by the Catholic community as a definite campaign to gain control of the area. (This is typical of many beliefs about action supposedly organized by the Bishop, or the Cardinal Archbishop of Armagh, or even by the Pope himself; but it is worth noting that local gossip has it that the Unionist Party has funds for the same purpose.) Catholic land, it is said, rarely comes upon the market; on the other hand the Catholic community collects funds which form the basis of loans for the purchase of land previously held by Protestants. A man in a certain area was known to have purchased land outside his means, and to have said that he could not have done so without 'the help of the Church'. This was taken to mean that the fund was officially organized by the Church itself, although this could not be proved. But people think that care will stop things going wrong. 'Both groups have their own auctioneers who are expected to know all the people over a wide area. Should the highest bid come from the wrong side they declare that the property has not realized its reserve, and ask for tenders to be submitted by post.'[4]

[4] R. L. Harris, unpublished London University M.A. thesis, p. 216.

The 'I.R.A.' outbreaks of violence[5] against Customs installations and police barracks increased the tension in the Border areas. It is generally agreed that these acts made singularly little impact on relationships in the Belfast area, and some country-dwellers maintain that Belfast wrote them off too lightly, and that in certain areas their women folk were afraid to go out at night. There was a nagging feeling that perhaps after all your Catholic neighbour might have given shelter to arms or to 'raiders'. There remains also some Catholic uneasiness over the existence of the auxiliary force, the 'B' Specials, recruited in practice exclusively from Protestants. These paid part-time policemen may be a farmer's neighbours by day, but at night they become men armed with rifles who have the right to stop and question anyone.

Reference has already been made to the Orange Order and its religious significance. Both this movement and a Catholic order, the Ancient Order of Hibernians, tend to increase group awareness in the countryside and to keep alive divisions in social life as well as in the religious and political spheres. The attitude to the Orange Order varies in different areas. In some the social pressure on Protestants to join the Order is strong, and in these districts membership is drawn from all parts of the social scale. However, in general, there is little support from the higher income groups, and practically none from professional men and intellectuals, who tend to look upon the Order as an antiquated, intolerant, and reactionary group. An exception to this is that almost all those with Unionist political ambitions find it necessary to join the Order, and to lend their patronage, so as to show beyond all shadow of a doubt where they stand on the constitutional and religious issues. All or almost all members of the Government are believed to be 'Orangemen'; even the Speaker of the House of Commons is Imperial Sovereign Grand Master of the Royal Black Institution, a body similar to the Orange Order. Complaint is made by members of the Order that many Protestants scorn the Lodges, and yet turn to them in time of need (in the years 1920–1922 for instance). There is probably some truth in this, in that some who regard the Order as beneath their intellectual or social dignity are glad enough that it exists as a form of 'Home

[5] See p. 130.

Guard' reserve, to rally Protestant opinion to the colours when necessary. Others regard the Order as rather an embarrassment—an intransigent over-statement of their case which serves only to impede the election of tolerant and forward-looking men to the Unionist Party. Such an attitude would, however, be more common in the towns than in the country, where tolerance is hardly likely to have a high status as a group virtue.

The Ancient Order of Hibernians fulfils a somewhat similar function within the Catholic community, but has not the same political influence, and cannot be said to be a significant initiating force in Nationalist politics. But even if the minority position of the Catholic community were not a sufficient factor to ensure group awareness, the fact that in a rural area Catholics attend only one place of worship, as compared to the Protestant with his several denominations, and belong to a Church which makes such distinct claims on social life, would in any case ensure a communal spirit.

The cleric, particularly in rural areas, receives much respect, and can still today wield considerable influence. A recent example of this was in Dungiven, a small town in Co. Londonderry with a strong Catholic majority, some of whose more unruly elements (reinforced from the neighbouring areas) were demonstrating against an Orange Lodge band which was marching through the town. There had been a skirmish on a similar occasion in 1958, and in 1959 the Minister for Home Affairs, Colonel Topping, forbade the band to march through the town. The prohibition was lifted in 1960 by a new Minister, Mr. Faulkner, and the local opposition was in wait for the band, which they claimed was marching merely to annoy them. Extra police were drafted in, but when it looked as if an ugly scene might occur the parish priest and his curate arrived on the scene and successfully called upon their people to disperse—not an easy achievement when a mob's blood is up.

In the small country villages and towns there is a certain amount of intervisitation between the Protestant denominations, especially at Harvest Thanksgiving time. When it comes to fund-raising sales, fêtes, and bazaars, there is generous cross-support, and this covers Catholic functions also. This is possibly due to the fact that there are not so many alternative attractions in a country district, and consequently these functions are highlighted in a way which would not be possible in a larger town. It has been said to us that often it seems that each citizen is responsible for maintaining churches and halls of the other principal denominations as well as his own. The need for such support is illustrated by one small village with a population of 192 (in the 1951 Census), but serving a large rural area, which has recently been active in modernizing and repairing three church halls, together with an Orange hall and a British Legion hall, to say nothing of repairs to a diocesan Cathedral of the Church of Ireland. The Catholic community, as in so many other areas, are also raising funds for a new secondary school.

Weddings and funerals are attended by both Protestants and Catholics, but it is only on unusual occasions that one will enter the other's church for the service. The extent of co-operation depends on the attitudes of the local clergy. Where there is a keen 'Orange' parson mutual help might be frowned upon and the relationship with the parish priest be merely one of formal politeness; and the same might be true if the priest is narrow in his outlook. Sometimes, however, priest and parson are close friends and co-operation is encouraged. The parish priest has the greater social influence with his flock and therefore takes the lead in determining the amount of social co-operation in Protestant or non-Catholic activities. If he fears proselytism in almost every non-Catholic activity, then Catholics who attend some cultural or social activity organized outside their Church mysteriously drop away, leaving perhaps one or two independent-minded people. Protestants do not attend many Catholic activities, because usually these are exclusively Church affairs. Dances run by the Catholic community are an exception, and there are a number of Protestants who enjoy the traditional (or pseudo-traditional) Irish dances. Some Protestants go to Catholic 'concerts' or dances held on a Sunday in a nearby town (where their presence is not so noticeable)—not because they have any particular desire to show goodwill or co-operation but because there is nowhere else to go. This, of course, is severely frowned upon by the majority of the Protestant community on the double count of breaking the Sabbath and of letting down one's own side.

Some attempts at proselytizing do take place, by travelling colporteurs (who sell or give away tracts and Bibles)—usually belonging to small evangelical (sometimes inter-denominational) sects and movements—and by the Jehovah's Witnesses. Tent and open-air 'Missions' are held, but these are mainly for the 'unsaved' Protestant. We hear very little about Catholic proselytizing. There is indeed an annual series of lectures in Belfast for 'non-Catholics', organized by the Clonard Monastery, and the Legion of Mary holds public meetings on occasion and has stalls for the sale of literature. On the whole in rural areas there is a strict code of respect for the other man's right to follow his religious observances; Catholics are expected to attend Mass when it is required of them and nothing is done to impede them, and Catholics respect Protestant churches and the Protestant's church attendance, even if they feel that strict Sabbatarianism is straining at a gnat.

There are, of course, local variations in the relations we have described, between different parts of Ulster, although the difference is of degree rather than of kind. In Co. Antrim, particularly on the north-east coast, the Catholics may come from families of note who have inhabited the 'Glens' for generations. After 1641 and through the Penal Code days they may have changed their name to a 'Protestant' one, but sometimes the original name was remembered and used amongst themselves, and the old name was brought into use again after the Emancipation Act. Catholics in this area tend to be of a higher social standing, with more local pride and self-assurance, and in the past there was a considerable amount of intermarrying, so that most families will have had some ancestor of the other religious group. There were a number of church schools attended by members of the other faith. There has thus been more of a tradition of ready co-operation. This should not be over-stressed, for since the establishment of Northern Ireland and the development of more educational segregation the picture has, we are told, changed somewhat.

2. The Provincial Towns

Apart from Belfast and Londonderry (the latter with a population of about 54,000) the towns of Ulster are small; next in size come Newtownabbey, a suburb of Belfast (about 37,000), and Bangor, a seaside resort and dormitory town for Belfast (about 24,000), followed by Portadown, Lurgan, Lisburn, Larne,

Ballymena, Newtownards, Newry, Coleraine, and Carrickfergus (between 10,000 and 20,000), and Armagh, Omagh, Holywood, Strabane, Enniskillen, Dungannon, and Banbridge (between 5,000 and 10,000). Although they may look similar to a visitor, the towns have considerable individuality, created by their various geographical positions and economic functions, by their past history, and by the balance between the different religious groups within them. Thus we have:

Protestant majority, largest Protestant group from Church of Ireland:

Portadown, Lurgan, Lisburn (three towns along the Lagan valley); Coleraine, Holywood.

Protestant majority, largest Protestant group from Presbyterian Church:

Ballymena, Ballymoney, Larne (towns in Co. Antrim); Bangor, Newtownards.

Roman Catholic majority, largest Protestant group from Church of Ireland:

Ballycastle (in the Catholic area of Co. Antrim); Armagh (the ecclesiastical capital); Downpatrick, Enniskillen, Dungannon, Omagh. In Newry over 80 per cent of the population is Catholic, and the Church of Ireland and the Presbyterians are about equal in strength.

Roman Catholic majority, largest Protestant group from Presbyterian Church:

Londonderry, Strabane.

Closer examination reveals other differences; for instance, Ballymoney has a reputation for its liberal, radical, and co-operative spirit, which was shown in the life of the great Minister of its Second Presbyterian Church, J. B. Armour; Bangor is a stronghold of Evangelical and fundamentalist thought; Portadown is a considerable centre of Methodism, which claims about one in seven of the town's inhabitants. In five of the towns the ratio of Catholics to Protestants lies not far from parity; these towns are Ballycastle (59 to 41), Armagh (57 to 43), Enniskillen (56 to 44),

Dungannon (52 to 48), and Lurgan (43 to 57),[6] and in these towns rivalry is naturally liable to be more intense.

In the towns local government affairs are of more direct and immediate interest than in the country. The local Council is a source of jobs, of contracts, and of houses; the latter in particular are important to those who live in towns and have no land of their own. It is generally expected that local government bodies in Ulster will favour those of the religious group which elected them.[7] This expectation has an important effect on local relations between the two communities.

Thus in Newry, whose Urban Council formerly had a majority of Nationalists under the title of the Irish Citizens' Association, and now has a majority from the Eire Labour Party, it is accepted as inevitable that there will be some sort of Catholic control, and social tensions do not appear to be acute despite the existence of over 15 per cent unemployment. The Council employees are nearly all Catholic; according to a statement made in the Senate in 1958, out of 765 Council houses, 743 were occupied by Catholics and 22 by Protestants. (The number of Protestant-occupied houses would be about 135 if they held houses in proportion to their numbers.) But the Council's answer is that the economic position of Catholics is so much worse than that of Protestants that it is natural and just that they should receive preference, both in employment and in housing. Houses are in fact allocated by a points system based on need.

In Londonderry, on the other hand, the City Council has a Protestant and Unionist majority of 12 to 8 ruling a population more than half Catholic. Catholics are not employed at the Guildhall, though they work on Council projects elsewhere in the city. Even in Londonderry, more than two houses have been built for Catholic occupation to every one for Protestants, but the siting of new houses has to be arranged with great care if it is not to upset the Unionist majority.[8] A prominent Unionist told us that Catholic housing needs were great, but this (he said) was because the Catholic Church encourages people to have families far larger than they can rear. He did not see why Protestants should be expected to find capital to build houses for such

[6] These ratios are from the 1951 Census, 1961 figures being so far unavailable.
[7] See p. 97.   [8] See p. 120.

families, and to subsidize their rents, so that Catholics could live in comfortable idleness on unemployment benefit and family allowances. The Protestants were being asked to subsidize an increase of population which would vote them out of control of their own money. Those who pay the piper should call the tune: 'that is true democracy, not the mere counting of heads'.

But there is more in Protestant feeling than the defence of property. The glories of Londonderry's history are proud Protestant memories; the city in its present form is an English and Protestant creation, and it would be a great blow to Protestant prestige to allow it to be ruled by its majority. The Nationalists might declare the city part of the Republic and fly the tricolour on the Guildhall; they would certainly (it is thought) discriminate as strongly against Protestants as Unionists have ever done against Catholics. On the other hand, the Catholic population of Londonderry feels itself to be deprived of control by gerrymandering (see p. 120), and reacts by non-co-operation and by unconstructive opposition. This in turn strengthens the Protestant will to hold on, by making plausible the argument that the Catholics are unfit to rule the city. Naturally in such a situation social divisions cut deep.

The pattern of urban living makes possible a degree of segregation which is greater than in the country, where one can hardly avoid knowing neighbours of both faiths for some distance around. Areas like the Creggan estate in Londonderry belong almost exclusively to Catholics. Segregation is increased by the political pressures, since a Unionist council will try to avoid putting Catholic tenants into a Unionist ward. Some local councils award both houses and jobs on a canvassing system; the applicant is given a list of Councillors or committee members, and is expected to visit them to plead his case. Such a method naturally brings political and religious considerations to the forefront of people's minds, and, even if it does not always in fact lead to a preference being given to the religious majority on grounds of religion, it is bound to leave the suspicion of favouritism.

So far we have suggested various ways in which the influences of urban living are likely to increase social divisions and antagonisms, unless one community has a large and unquestioned majority and control. Against this we must set the anonymity of urban life (a still more important influence in Belfast, of course). In the country a man's opinions and actions are known, and any crossing of lines of division will be noticed at once; in the town a Protestant can go to a Catholic dance-hall on Sunday (for instance) without the same danger of attracting notice. Non-sectarian activities such as those of the Workers' Educational Association can draw members from both communities; though in Londonderry even this has proved difficult.

The towns are also the centre of a professional and business life which employs some Catholics at a social and economic level which raises them above the conflict. If there are only a few big houses, the well-to-do Catholic can hardly live a segregated life; and, indeed, he may have no desire to do so, preferring to be a respected member of the town's upper class, with many Protestant friends, perhaps membership of the Rotary Club, and week-ends on the golf course. Some Catholics are inhibited in making such contacts, even if their social position permits, because of their Nationalist connexions and traditions; others are assisted by having served under the British Crown in the Forces or elsewhere. We find that on going to a provincial town we are referred time and time again to the same small group of Catholics, as being 'interested in co-operation'; and most of these will be professional and business men of liberal outlook. It is sometimes possible to identify a similar group of Protestants with a liberal interest in Irish Nationalism; but this is the outlook of an older generation, and we find that the younger Protestants, in the higher social classes, while not liking a display of political sentiment (and perhaps making fun of the Orange Order) take the British connexion very much for granted. If there is to be any bridge-building, they expect it to start from the Catholic side.

We shall have occasion in later chapters to mention other instances of social tension or division in provincial towns—for example, opposition to C.E.M.A. (the equivalent to the Arts Council) because the National Anthem has to be played at performances which it sponsors (p. 145): and segregation in sports clubs (p. 148). A Catholic in Portadown told us that he had stopped attending the Junior Chamber of Commerce because, as the only Catholic there, he felt 'out of things'; the incident is typical of the awkwardness of relations. On the other hand, we have found various instances of co-operation, even in the unpromising surroundings of Londonderry, in social work and games. But much of the co-operation which exists does not touch the ordinary man in the street.

3. The City of Belfast

Belfast is a large city, of half a million people, crowded by the hills into a narrow site. It is a great industrial centre, with a strong trade union movement, and this introduces an industrial interest which to some extent cuts across the line of religious division (p. 138). The opportunities for contact among the business and professional classes are perhaps larger here, where there are so many more such people; on the other hand, bigger numbers make it easier for the Catholic professional man (for instance) to meet mainly his Catholic colleagues. The size of the place increases the opportunities given by anonymity, and it provides a more promising ground for independent radical thought, for the 'odd man out' who has broken away from the narrow sectarian line. Art, music, drama have a more central place, and offer a uniting interest. The University, the chief centre of non-sectarian education in the Province, has an influence in lessening divisions; and (like the senior ranks of the Civil Service and of some large business firms) it tends to draw staff from other parts of the United Kingdom.

On balance, these are influences which narrow the divisions between the two communities. Local government, firmly in Unionist hands, does not in Belfast excite the passions felt in smaller towns. The greater size of the place means more stress on technical skill of administration, and less on personal and political issues, and the City Council is a distant body which one reads about in the newspapers but whose members one probably would not recognize in the street. But segregation in housing is as clear in Belfast as anywhere in the Province; and, against all the uniting influences, one must set the fact that in a great city a man can find all the friends and all the services he needs without going beyond casual contact with those of another faith.

All future analysis of the social situation in Belfast will owe much to the work of Dr. Emrys Jones during his tenure of a post in the Geography Department of the Queen's University. We are grateful for permission to draw freely from Dr. Jones's detailed study.[9] He points out that although discrimination was not required by the Charter by which Belfast became a Borough in 1613, it appears that for the next hundred years or so the native Irish were forced to live outside the city walls. There had been for long a Catholic parish at Derriaghy, some six miles distant up the Lagan valley, and it was along the approach from this south-west area along the northern flanks of the valley, known as the Falls district, that the Catholic families congregated. The community established itself in the expanding town around what was then known as Mill Street; and today this area from Divis Street and Millfield to what was known as the Pound Loney remains very strongly Catholic, as is the whole Falls Road approach. It was in the Mill Street area that in 1783 the first Catholic church was built in Belfast since Reformation times, and the Volunteers (a largely Presbyterian body, forerunner of the United Irishmen) subscribed to its building and paraded for its opening.

The Catholic population grew with the rapid industrial development of Belfast in the first half of the last century, so that by the 1861 Census it had reached 34 per cent of the whole, the highest proportion so far attained. By this date the divisions were hardening in Ulster, and there had already been some sectarian rioting in Belfast in 1857. Riots were part of the pattern of life in the second half of the century—they occurred in 1857, 1864, 1872, and then (intensified by the Home Rule struggle) in 1886, 1893, and 1898.

Whereas the Catholic workers lived along the Falls approach, the Protestant workers lived along what was then the main road to Dublin and the south, an area generally known as Sandy Row. There was a preponderance of Church of Ireland members in this district, while in the north, in the Shankill and Crumlin Road areas, the Presbyterians (from Co. Antrim) were in the majority. To the east of the Lagan River the people were (and are) mostly Protestant, although there is a small concentration of Catholic workers in the Ballymacarrett area, and just across the river another group in what is known as the Markets area. The centre of the city is very low-lying and was formerly subject to flooding, especially

[9] *A Social Geography of Belfast* (Oxford University Press, 1960). See also an article in the *Sociological Review*, December 1956, pp. 167–89.

from the Blackstaff River. Consequently when the upper-class homes, which used to surround the old Linen Hall in Donegall Square and which spread along Donegall Place and Castle Place, started to give way to shops, banks, and offices, the low-lying slob-land was by-passed and the new homes for the wealthy were built on the sounder and healthier Malone Ridge to the south-west or on the slopes of Cave Hill to the north, or the sand and gravels of the Knock and Rosetta areas to the east and south-east.

The pattern of segregated living can be roughly seen in the following analysis of population on a ward basis, as given by the 1951 Census returns:

Analysis by Religions of the Population of Electoral Wards in Belfast, 1951

Ward	Roman Catholic %	Presby- terian %	Church of Ireland %	Metho- dist %	Others %
Clifton . .	33·9	28·8	24·3	6·5	6·5
Court . .	24·4	29·7	40·0	3·2	2·7
Cromac . .	23·9	30·2	31·1	7·9	6·9
Dock . .	50·1	19·6	19·9	7·4	3·0
Duncairn . .	13·1	40·7	28·4	10·9	6·7
Falls . .	92·8	2·2	3·2	3·2	0·7
Ormeau . .	9·7	41·0	28·3	10·0	11·0
Pottinger . .	14·6	36·6	32·0	8·2	9·0
St. Anne's . .	40·7	20·8	27·0	8·0	3·5
St. George's .	4·5	29·5	49·8	11·4	4·8
Shankill . .	6·4	37·2	39·2	10·3	6·9
Smithfield . .	91·2	1·3	6·7	0·2	0·6
Victoria . .	5·2	37·3	42·2	8·1	7·2
Windsor . .	15·5	35·5	33·3	8·7	7·0
Woodvale . .	7·8	36·9	41·2	9·4	4·7
Total for City .	25·9	30·4	29·7	7·8	6·2

The total population was 443,671.

This table shows a considerable variation between the different wards, the pattern being set by the general geographical development as we have outlined it above. The considerable degree of segregation is shown by the fact that there were seven of the fifteen wards with over 90 per cent of the population belonging to one or other of the two main religious divisions, two Catholic and five Protestant. The highest concentration, 95·5 per cent, was of Protestants in the small St. George's Ward in the centre of the town, which includes also the Sandy Row area. Next came an area of somewhat mixed social class, Victoria, covering the eastern shore approaches, and having 94·8 per cent of Protestants.

This does not include an 'ancient' Protestant sector, but is rather an area of growth where Catholics had not penetrated. Woodvale and Shankill to the north and Ormeau to the south-east were two other electoral districts with a Protestant concentration of over 90 per cent. The area with the greatest divergence from the average (only 25·9 per cent of the city was Catholic) was in the Falls district, where the concentration was 92·8 per cent of the Catholic faith. Smithfield, which includes the bottom end of the Falls area, where the Falls Road runs into Divis Street, and also the famous Pound Loney, is a small ward (only 10,539 inhabitants), but had 91·2 per cent of Catholics. The second largest Catholic group by numbers was in a huge ward running from the working-class Crumlin Road, through an area of high-class housing in decay, into a high social class living area on the city boundary. There were 17,465 Catholics in this 'Clifton' Ward, though this represents a percentage of only 33·9. In the smaller working-class central area called 'Dock Ward' there were 50·1 per cent Catholics.

While this ward analysis gives a good general picture, Dr. Jones was able to make a much more detailed analysis by working on a basis of the 231 enumeration districts. He took these groups (of about 2,000 people), being those in the area allotted to each Enumeration Officer in making the Census in 1951, and found the religious proportions for each. These he compares with the socio-economic rating for each district, found by grouping the workers by occupation into five groups according to skill and responsibility, and summarizing the proportions in index form. Using this comparison, Dr. Jones was able to draw maps showing the segregation of the religious and social strata with much greater accuracy, since the wards are too large to reveal small pockets of high density grouping, and they do not show areas of segregation which overrun an electoral boundary.

As well as showing a high degree of correlation between low socio-economic rating and a high proportion of Catholics, Dr. Jones has revealed some interesting differences between the leading Protestant groups. The density of Presbyterians is higher than that of the Church of Ireland members, and significantly so, in the higher-rated social areas which fall along the Malone 'ridge', in the Knock area to the south-east, and on the Castlereagh hill slopes, as well as being higher (as would be expected from the nearness to the Antrim countryside) along the Shore and Antrim Roads. The members of the Church of Ireland are drawn from a lower income group on the average, and this is reflected in the high Church of Ireland concentration in the Court (lower Crumlin–Shankill Roads), St. George's, and Smithfield Wards. Such a social grouping is interesting because in the country areas the landed proprietors are often drawn from the Church of Ireland. It looks as though, while the gentry remained on the land, the poorer Church of Ireland members migrated to the city as industrial workers, whereas (as in England) more Non-conformists were successful in commerce and established themselves among the wealthy urban families.

Like other cities, Belfast is embedded in a larger conurbation, now of around 600,000 population. The 1951 Census returns analyse a part of the additional population, to a number of 54,424, living in residential areas outside the city boundary but more or less continuous with the city's housing. This population showed, compared with the city area, a lower proportion of Catholics (20·5 per cent) and a higher proportion of Presbyterians (35·4 per cent), no doubt a reflection of the higher social status and higher cost of suburban living. The present position is uncertain, since some estates of subsidized housing, with many Catholic tenants, have been built outside the city during the last decade.

As often happens in great cities, small areas develop a clannishness which is not necessarily a result of the religious segregation. On this subject F. A. W. Carter[10] writes:

'It cannot be over-emphasised that the people of the Loney [this is the Pound Loney mentioned above] are conscious that they live in a distinct section of the town. Those who attempt to cross the boundaries, whether in applying for a new house or new employment, or simply in walking in the streets of another part of the town, are made aware that their origin sets them at a disadvantage. The response is withdrawal to the familiar streets of the Loney. There are many stories of families who move out to the comparative comfort of the newly-built housing estates, only to return to the over-crowded Loney after a short stay.'

[10] *Juvenile Delinquency Areas of Belfast*, unpublished B. Ed. dissertation, Queen's University, 1953.

We have heard confirmation of this, and of some young wives in the newer areas who, when they have got their husbands off to work and the children off to school, return with the younger children to the city streets, and to their parents, aunts, and old neighbours, for the old familiar 'crack' and gossip. This resistance to new areas is a class phenomenon rather than a sectarian one, but the influence on sectarianism is obvious—that the divisions tend to be perpetuated. If a family feels very much a part of its old city area, and if unity in church connexion was part of the area's flavour, then at least the family will try to transplant the same sectarian feeling to a new area of residence so that it can feel more at home. We have heard of families moving to a new housing area where they are in a religious minority, and shortly afterwards arranging to move again to another new estate where they were surrounded by a majority of their own religious group. The instances most often quoted relate to moves from the Corporation's Highfield estate to the almost 100 per cent Catholic Ballymurphy estate or (for a better type of housing) to the Housing Trust dwellings at Andersonstown. On occasions, when a Catholic wishes to move to a better dwelling, he must move into a Protestant area; but this is not so obvious in Belfast, where the number of Catholics is large enough to support better-class Catholic housing. Houses of professional class valuation exist on the Falls Road outside the city boundary. We are told, however, that the Catholic proportion in the high-class Antrim Road district has increased of late, and that many Catholics are 'up-grading' into this area; it is already the home district for the majority of Belfast's 1,140 Jews, and it contains their synagogue and Institute.

A few Protestants in a Catholic majority area may feel particularly isolated, because they are split up between several denominations, whereas the Catholics will meet each other at Mass. This is, however, less important than it appears, because of the lively social life within the Protestant churches. Attendance at church is the normal and accepted thing; congregations are commonly of a considerable size, and can thus support a wide range of ancillary activities, such as women's guilds, youth groups, badminton clubs, and men's discussion fellowships. In a distinct but important part of society, the frequent evangelical campaigns help people to retain the sense of active belonging. But the way is not wholly smooth for a member of either community if he is surrounded by people of the opposite belief. On an occasion such as the Queen's Coronation, for instance, was he to fly the Union Jack, the papal colours, or no flag at all? Any of these courses would be liable to annoy somebody.

It must continually be remembered that the local loyalties which would occur in any large city will in Belfast tend to be expressed in the language of the sectarian conflict. Thus we are told that the various juvenile gangs, such as the 'Loneys' from the Pound Loney, the 'Marketers', and the 'Ivy Boys' from the lower Ravenhill area, use a question about religion as a kind of pass-word. However, there is no doubt that (although the old catch-phrases may still be used) people are in practice more willing to 'live and let live' than they were in the past. A common memory in Belfast is of lying on the floor of a tram-car to avoid bullets during the 'Troubles' of 1920-21; in 1935 serious riots were started by the march of an Orange band in the Markets area of the city. In July 1959, following a meeting sponsored by Ulster Protestant Action, a few stones were thrown at Catholic shops; but the trouble quickly died down, without reprisals. Catholics will now enter the Sandy Row area to look for jobs, whereas forty years ago (we are told) they would not even walk through it. Catholics now shop in the Protestant area of the Shankill Road, because it is known to be a good shopping centre; and (of course) the growth of great impersonal multiple firms is breaking down the old tendency to 'buy only from one's own people'.

The high-water mark of co-operation is perhaps to be found among University students. Seventy-eight per cent of those questioned in our student survey claimed friendships with those of the opposite faith. These are high figures, considering that educational segregation before the university stage is almost complete. The students were not unaware of the dangers of such friendship; 96 per cent of them considered (with varying degrees of firmness) that mixed marriages should be avoided. Perhaps in later life most of them will follow the general pattern of segregated living; but at least some bonds must have been created which will endure. In later chapters we shall note a number of other instances where the diversity of city life allows the creation of valuable social relationships, across the lines of religious division.

CHAPTER 5

EDUCATION AND THE SECTARIAN PROBLEM

A CHILD in Northern Ireland will become conscious that all children are not like himself at a very early age; he may be discouraged from playing with the children of a neighbour of different religion, and he is almost certain to hear grown-ups speaking of people according to their religious allegiance. But from the age of five the difference becomes obvious, as he sets out for a different school, where he is likely in future to find most or all of his friends and playmates. Many Protestants have spoken to us of separate education as a basic cause of friction and division. In a few country places, schools are still mixed, and we hear such remarks as: 'He is not nearly as bitter as some Roman Catholics; he went to school with Protestants.' A Protestant who attended a mixed school in the north of County Antrim said that there was no sense of division—the Catholics were regarded with some envy because they had the privilege of being excused from Scripture classes.

We have not found Catholics ready to express the same concern about the divisive influence of separate education. As in other countries, they for the most part assume that, as a natural consequence of their faith, their children must go to Catholic schools; and this not only because of denominational teaching, but because the whole atmosphere of the school helps the children to withstand materialist influences. We are told that some Catholic parents do not like their children even to play with Protestants 'because of the lack of morals and the bad language they might pick up'.

In 1960, 41 per cent of the school population was Catholic, and 59 per cent Protestant; these figures may be compared with a division of the *whole* population of about 35 to 65. As far as can be discovered, at least 98 per cent (and probably more) of all Catholic primary school children attend Catholic schools. The history of this segregation is, however, by no means as straightforward as many people now suppose. We therefore summarize its main points.

Before 1831 those children in Ulster who received any education went for the most part to small single-teacher schools, averaging about forty pupils each. These were run either by a local church (with the minister or priest as manager) or as a private venture by the schoolmaster, who might supplement his meagre income from fees by occasional grants from educational charities. Such schools provided much of what we now call 'secondary' education, as well as the elementary stages, for the 'Royal' schools in Ireland, endowed by the Stuarts, met only a small part of the need. In 1810 the Presbyterian community in Belfast had endowed the Academical Institution, to act both as a school for boys and as what might now be described as a 'liberal arts college' on the American definition. At this Institution Presbyterian ministers, who previously had been forced to seek their higher education at the University of Glasgow or (after 1793) at Trinity College, Dublin, could study to a standard recognized by their Church as equivalent to a first degree, before going elsewhere for a two-year divinity course. Catholic priests, until the late eighteenth century mostly educated at Paris, Rome, or Louvain, were after 1795 able to go to the college at Maynooth; it is said that in the early days a few priests received their first-degree training at the Belfast Academical Institution before proceeding to Maynooth.

The year 1811 saw the founding in Dublin of the 'Society for promoting the education of the poor in Ireland', otherwise known as the Kildare Place Society; and from 1815 this Society received grants from Parliament which were applied for the assistance of local schools. It had the object of affording 'the same advantages to all classes of professing Christians without interfering with the peculiar religious opinions of any'; for a period its schools were largely attended by Catholic children, but the Society's method of reading the Bible 'without note or comment' was not acceptable to the priests, and the Kildare Place system aroused increasing opposition. A petition from 'the Prelates of the Roman Catholic Church in Ireland' to the House of Commons in 1824 explains the situation:

'The Petitioners beg leave most respectfully to submit to the House, that in the Roman Catholic Church the literary and religious instruction of youth are universally combined . . . that the religious instruction of youth in Catholic schools is always conveyed by means of catechistical instruction, daily prayer, and the reading of religious books, wherein the Gospel Morality is explained and inculcated; that Roman Catholics have ever considered the reading of the sacred Scriptures by children as an inadequate means of imparting to them religious instruction, as a usage whereby the word of God is made liable to irreverence (and) youth exposed to misunderstanding its meaning . . . that when the Petitioners learned, some years past, that the Legislature had granted a considerable sum of money for the purpose of promoting a well-ordered system of education in Ireland without religious instruction, they conceived the strongest hope that the money so granted would be fairly employed in providing for the education of the Roman Catholic poor, and that no regulations of a private or partial kind would be suffered to interfere with the benevolent intentions of the Legislature . . .'[1]

The views of the Catholic hierarchy on mixed education at this period are not clear—probably they were prepared to compromise because of the desperate needs of their people. But a more positive attitude was expressed by James Doyle, Bishop of Kildare and Leighlin, in these words:

'I do not see how any man, wishing well to the public peace, and who looks to Ireland as his country, can think that peace can ever be permanently established, or the prosperity of the country ever well secured, if children are separated, at the commencement of life, on account of their religious opinions. I do not know any measures which would prepare the way for a better feeling in Ireland than uniting children at an early age, and bringing them up in the same school, leading them to commune with one another, and to form those little intimacies and friendships which often subsist through life.'[2]

This view was also proclaimed by Thomas Wyse, M.P., Catholic and graduate of Trinity College, Dublin, who brought forward plans for a national system of education in Ireland. These plans, though not directly adopted, had an effect on the administration; in September 1831 the Chief Secretary, Stanley, announced the Government's intention of assuming direct responsibility for primary education, withdrawing support from the

[1] Quoted in *First Report of the Commissioners on Education in Ireland*, 1825, H.C. 1825 (400), xii, p. 1.

[2] Quoted in T. W. Moody and J. C. Beckett, *Queen's, Belfast*, vol. I, p. lvi, from *Second Report of Evidence from the Select Committee on the State of the Poor in Ireland*, H.C. 1830 (654), vii, pp. 426–7.

Kildare Place Society. He appointed a Board of seven Com
missioners of Education, two of whom were Catholics, with wid
powers of constructing schools, giving grants to teachers, appoint
ing inspectors, and publishing textbooks. Stanley's plan was 't
afford the people of Ireland the advantages of a combined literar
and separate religious education'; he instructed the Board tha
one of its first and fundamental obligations was the safeguardin
of the religion of the pupils. Religious instruction in the nev
'national schools' was to be given in separate groups, and with th
consent of the parents, by ministers, priests, or others accredite
by the various churches, who for this purpose were to have acces
to the schools.

Such a system implied that the Bible, which had previously bee
used as a kind of textbook for reading and English, would b
confined to the classes for religious instruction; and this rouse
Protestant opposition, since many Protestants felt that wisdom wa
learnt unconsciously from a general use of Holy Writ, and tha
even Catholic children should have a chance of hearing in un
tainted form the 'word of the living God'. In 1833 the Presbyteria
Synod of Ulster passed a resolution that it should be right fo
school managers and teachers to read the scriptures during schoo
hours. In 1839 a new principle was established; the Rev. Dr
Stewart of Broughshane near Ballymena made application that th
Presbyterian school at Correen should be taken over by the Com
missioners of Education on condition that there should be a righ
to read the scriptures during ordinary school hours (subject to
clause allowing parents to keep their children away from classe
where this was done): and a right also to refuse entrance to childre
of other denominations, which would enable the managers t
avoid the offence which would be caused if they had to admit
priest to give religious instruction to Catholics. The school wa
accepted on these conditions, and qualified for government grants

Protestant dissatisfaction with the national school system wa
shown by the foundation of the Education Society of the established Church of Ireland in 1838, to maintain schools independen
of the Board of Education. Catholic opinion was also dissatisfied
because 'combined literary and separate religious education' fel
short of the ideal of 'literary and religious instruction universall
combined'. In general, however, the rules of the Board were

adopted, and a system of education was created with two main elements: voluntary schools established by the churches, giving religious instruction according to the wishes of their managers, but with the State paying the salaries of most of the teachers; and 'model schools', built and maintained by the State, in which the principle was established that if six or more children (through their parents) demanded separate religious instruction a teacher would be provided to give this instruction in school hours. Thus the principles of segregation and of common education grew up side by side.

Educational services were transferred to the Northern Ireland Ministry of Education in Belfast on 1 February 1922, and a committee under the chairmanship of Sir Robert Lynn, M.P., was appointed to report on them and to recommend policy for the future. The Catholic community was not prepared to be represented on this committee. The Lynn Committee found that there was a large deficit of school places in Belfast, and unnecessary competition between numerous small denominational schools elsewhere; it recommended various measures of assistance, control, and co-ordination, but also the continuation of the previous arrangements for religious instruction. The Education Act of June 1923, however, attempted (with little regard for history) to avoid the thorny problems of religious instruction in normal school hours. This Act and a successor in 1925 provided for three main kinds of primary school: those to be wholly maintained by local authorities of Counties and County Boroughs, including any private or denominational schools which were transferred to 'wholly maintained' status; voluntary schools under what were called 'four and two committees'; and other voluntary schools. The 'four and two' committees consisted of four representatives of the body providing the school and two representatives of the local authority (so that denominational managers would have a majority in the running of their own schools). The 'four and two committee' schools qualified for a 100 per cent grant for teachers' salaries and for help with maintenance costs, and might at the discretion of the local authority receive capital grants also. Other voluntary schools qualified for help with salaries only.

Section 26 of the Act, however, stipulated that 'the education authority shall not provide religious instruction in any such public elementary school', and section 66 (3) that the 'religious denomination of a teacher must not be taken into account by the education authority when making an appointment'. Ministers of religion and other suitable persons were to have free access to teach the children for half an hour a day if the parents so desired; but any child could be excused from attending such classes. Religious instruction was thus to become an appendage of a secular education system, and not an integral part of it. The reason for these provisions was in part to keep open the possibility of a common education for Protestant and Catholic children. The Minister of Education, Lord Londonderry, is reported to have said at a conference with representatives of the Protestant churches 'that all the quarrels between Roman Catholics and Protestants arose out of the teaching of the Bible and as he wished the children of all denominations to meet in the same schools and grow up in a friendly atmosphere he thought this could only be achieved if there was no Bible instruction and if Roman Catholic and Protestant children mixed in the same schools'.[3] But another reason for the provisions may have been a desire to keep within the strict terms of section 5 of the Government of Ireland Act, which prohibits the endowment of any religion, and prohibits also any preference or privilege, or disability or disadvantage, to anyone on account of religious belief. It is clearly difficult to avoid preference if the State maintains schools which give religious instruction of a particular type.

It is probable that the secular education system proposed by the Act would even at that time have been wholly unacceptable to the Catholic hierarchy, despite the continuing need for improving the education of Catholics. It would certainly be unacceptable today.

'The Canon Law reads: "Parents have a most serious duty to secure a fully Catholic education for their children in all that concerns the instruction of their minds, the training of their wills to virtue, their bodily welfare and the preparation for their life as citizens."

'Again, it is decreed: "All the Faithful shall be so educated from childhood, that not only shall nothing contrary to the Catholic religion and good morals be taught them, but religious and moral education shall have the principal place. . . ."

[3] Very Rev. William Corkey, *Episode in the History of Protestant Ulster* (privately published pamphlet), p. 24.

'Lastly, the (Canon) law takes account of the dangers arising from non-Catholic schools: "Catholic pupils are not to frequent non-Catholic schools or neutral schools or schools that are open also to non-Catholics. Only the Ordinary of the place where the school is situated is competent to determine, according to the instructions of the Apostolic See, in what circumstances it may be tolerated for Catholics to attend such schools and what safeguards are to be prescribed against the danger of perversion . . ."

' . . . It is said that, in regard to youth, the Catholic Bishops are afraid. They are. But their fear is a solicitude, based on some two thousand years' experience. It is more fully based on their esteem for the priceless worth of sanctifying grace and the uniqueness of the one, true Faith. Therefore, they fear the circumstances that breed indifference and indiscipline.'[4]

It is clear from the tone of pronouncements such as this that permission to attend a non-Catholic place of education is to be granted only in very rare cases.

Whatever hopes of a mixed education Lord Londonderry may have entertained were in any case illusory after 1925, for in that year the Act was amended in a way which finally closed the door to a system of joint education. This amendment was necessary to meet the strong views of the Protestant majority; it followed a sustained campaign by a United Education Committee of the three main Protestant churches, in association with a committee of the Grand Orange Lodge of Ireland.

The Protestant argument was that they were being invited to transfer their voluntary schools to state control, on terms which would remove a most essential element from the curriculum, namely instruction in and through the Bible. They would not be able to ensure that teachers were qualified to teach Scripture, nor that they were of the same religious denomination as the parents of the children; and it was no answer to say that religious instruction could be provided by the ministers of religion, for in many areas pressure of work would render this impossible. Furthermore, in the Border areas, a wholly transferred Protestant school might come under the control of a Catholic County Council.

The Protestant campaign was thus on matters of deeply-held principle. 'Politicians are telling us', said Councillor Stewart at a

[4] From the Lenten Pastoral Letter of the Archbishop of Dublin, 1961 (M. H. Gill and Son, Dublin), with quotations from Canons 1113, 1372, and 1374.

conference called by the United Education Committee on 5 March 1925, 'that the Boundary question is more important than the question of the Bible in schools. But is not the Bible itself the boundary?' 'If there is an Ulster spirit,' said the Very Rev. Dean King of Londonderry at the same meeting, 'where does it come from? From the Bible, and not from the politicians—and now the Government are setting themselves to destroy the very principle that has made their existence possible.' 'The question is not merely for the clergy,' said Mrs. McGregor Greer of Carrickfergus, 'but for every God-fearing mother in Ulster. It is one that is too sacred for any heat to be shown, and if we desire peace and harmony in our Province how better bring that about than by teaching the Bible?'

On the day following this conference the Prime Minister, Sir James Craig, invited the secretaries of the United Committee and the Orange Order to meet him. He explained that 'as serious difficulties had arisen regarding the working of the Ministry of Education he as Prime Minister must assume reponsibility', and he had informed Lord Londonderry that he 'was negotiating regarding an amendment of the Education Act'.[5] St. John Ervine (in *Craigavon, Ulsterman*, p. 119) suggests that Sir James Craig had an antipathy to sectarian education, so that it appears that he was setting this on one side and overruling his own Minister for Education. He offered to delete the offending parts of sections 26 and 66(3), and this change was made by an Act passed a few days later (12 March 1925). Certain transitional difficulties remained, but the way was now open for the transfer of Protestant schools to the local authorities. Up to 1925 only ten Protestant schools (and no Catholic schools) had been transferred; by the end of 1927, 194 Protestant schools had been brought under local government control, and by the end of 1929, 440. The gaps in the Protestant primary education system were filled by government building of new 'provided' schools.

Difficulties were not, however, at an end. Certain restrictions on religious instruction had been removed, but nothing positive had been put in their place. The Ministry of Education still claimed that the Government of Ireland Act 'operates to prevent the Education Authorities . . . from applying public monies to the

[5] Corkey, op. cit., p. 44.

teaching of any particular religious beliefs or to the payment of salaries to persons who must be of a particular persuasion in schools under their management'.[6] The Ministry's case was weakened by the fact that grants were being paid in respect of students attending Catholic teachers' training colleges, and paid chaplains had been appointed to lecture on religious subjects to teachers in training at Stranmillis Training College, Belfast; but it was nevertheless based on a reasonable interpretation of the intention of the Government of Ireland Act.

After further pressure, the Ministry agreed that clauses might be inserted in the deeds of transfer of a school which would provide (a) for religious instruction by the teaching staff on a programme to be approved by the body transferring the school, and (b) for the cancellation of the transfer if a teacher was appointed who on religious grounds was objectionable to the persons transferring the school. This still left the problem of schools provided *ab initio* by the education authorities, and also the possibility of trouble between the churches and education authorities whose members were of a different persuasion. The 1930 Education Act dealt with these matters. Section 4 stated:

'It shall be the duty of the Education Authority to provide Bible instruction, should the parents of not less than ten children . . . make application to the Education Authority for that purpose. Where the Education Authority make arrangements for Bible instruction in a provided or transferred school it shall be the duty of the teachers of the school to give such instruction if so required by the Education Authority.'

The Act also provided for representation of 'transferors' on the Borough and Regional Education Committees. In answer to some questions on behalf of Protestant school managers who had lingering doubts, the Prime Minister (Lord Craigavon) stated that: 'The only thing that could bring about the repeal of this Education Act would be the coming into power in Northern Ireland of a Sinn Fein Government.'[7]

The Catholic community now considered its action in refusing to contemplate the transfer of its schools as fully justified, since

---

[6] Letter of 6 May 1925, quoted in Corkey, op. cit., p. 47.
[7] Corkey, op. cit., p. 88.

the State schools, whether transferred or provided, had now (in Catholic eyes) become Protestant schools. On the other hand, the Protestant view was that the changes were the least which were necessary to satisfy them on an important matter of religious principle. But it was also clear that the Government had to do something about the provision of new Catholic schools, which could not be left entirely to private charity. The 1930 Act therefore provided for grants of 50 per cent of the cost of approved capital works in a recognized voluntary or non-transferred school. These grants were increased to 65 per cent in 1947. The intermediate class of school, under a 'four and two committee', did not turn out in practice to be a satisfactory compromise. In January 1961 there were 91 schools with this status, mostly very small, and containing only 1,049 Catholic and 4,373 Protestant pupils. The difficulty seems to have been in part a suspicion of the local authority nominees; clerical managers of the schools were not anxious to have to work with 'outsiders' even if they were of the same religion. Some schools have also been transferred from 'four and two' status because they needed rebuilding or expansion. There were 1,272 Protestant pupils attending wholly voluntary primary schools (out of more than 103,000); and 879 Catholic pupils attending County primary schools (out of 90,000). Broadly speaking, therefore, Protestants were being educated in State schools and Catholics in voluntary schools. As mentioned earlier, a small number of 'mixed' schools still survive in country areas.

The settlement of 1930 was, despite Lord Craigavon's words, rudely shaken in 1944, when the Minister (Colonel Hall-Thompson) indicated his intention of repealing the religious instruction sections in the 1930 Education Act, on the grounds that they involved compulsion on teachers to give Bible instruction, and that there were doubts about the legality of the sections under the Government of Ireland Act. The policy of following Westminster 'step by step' in any case now required a recasting of the educational system. The 1947 Act in fact contained a small retreat towards a secular education system; teachers were to be excused from giving religious instruction on grounds of their religious belief, and they were not to suffer any loss of promotion or other advantage in consequence. Since it was also provided that ability to give religious instruction was not to be taken into account when making an appointment, a possibility was created (happily normally only a slight one) that a small school, originally a Church foundation, might find itself without any teachers willing to give simple Bible instruction. On the other hand it was provided that there should be 'collective worship' in the County schools, and also 'undenominational religious instruction', so that it was plainly the duty of education authorities to arrange matters so that this worship and instruction would be possible, if necessary by appointing an additional teacher (section 24(5)).

So far we have been discussing the broad base of the education system in the primary and all-age schools. This was almost all that existed at the foundation of the Northern Ireland Ministry of Education, there being in October 1921 only 6,237 secondary pupils. In January 1961 there were 84,128 (excluding the preparatory departments of grammar schools). The structure of the system is similar to that in England, but voluntary grammar schools have a higher importance:

January 1961		Number of Schools	Pupils (thousands)
Grammar Schools			
County	21		
Voluntary	60	81	32·5
Secondary Intermediate (= Modern) Schools			
County	64		
Voluntary	36	100	47·2
Technical Intermediate (= Technical) Schools (all County)		33	4·5
		214	84

Source: *Report of the Ministry of Education, 1960–61*

The broad picture is that the voluntary secondary intermediate schools are Catholic, while Protestants go to the County schools; about half the voluntary grammar schools (but with only a third of the pupils) are Catholic; the County grammar school pupils are almost all Protestant. The technical intermediate schools, however, are mixed and their position is further discussed below.

Of the pupils at grammar schools, 27 per cent are Roman Catholics, well below the population proportion, and still further below the proportion appropriate to the grammar school age group. This reflects the lower economic status of the Catholic population, as well as the difficulty in providing enough places by voluntary effort. Of the secondary intermediate school population, 30 per cent is Catholic; this figure is also low, because some Catholic children attend all-age schools which are included in the primary school total, and others attend technical schools because no secondary intermediate school is available in their area. It is not known how far the figures are further depressed by early leaving by Catholic children, but one would certainly expect this as a consequence of relative poverty.

The voluntary grammar schools are classified in two groups, 43 in group A and 17 in group B. A *group A school* places 80 per cent of its places at the disposal of the Ministry for pupils who have passed the Qualifying (i.e. 'eleven plus') Examination; it obtains salary and capitation grants towards its current expenses, and also 65 per cent of its approved capital costs. A *group B school* has no obligation about the pupils whom it takes, and gets no help towards capital costs; but it still obtains salary and capitation grants. Both Catholic and non-Catholic schools are to be found in both groups, the need to obtain the 65 per cent grant having in many cases overcome doubts about government interference. Local education authorities do not, of course, attempt to require qualified Protestant pupils to attend a Catholic school, or Catholic pupils to attend a non-Catholic school.

The technical intermediate schools spring from the strong Irish tradition of vocational education, and many of them were originally junior departments of technical colleges. Technical education at the higher levels has been regarded as outside the sectarian controversy, and the technical schools have in consequence remained mixed, in relation both to their pupils and to their staff and governing bodies. On the whole the schools appear to work well, though we are told that in some areas most Catholic pupils will be withdrawn when secondary intermediate school places are available.

A small amount of 'mixing' also takes place in voluntary grammar schools; thus the Rainey Endowed School at Magherafelt usually has some Catholics on the staff and a few Catholic pupils, and the same occurs in some Belfast schools. An occasional Protestant teacher is to be found in a Catholic school, perhaps as a stop-gap or as part-time teacher of a special subject. On the whole, however, there is little blurring of the hard edges of segregation. In this connexion it must be remembered that Protestant secondary school teachers will normally have obtained qualifications in Northern Ireland or in Great Britain, but that a sizeable proportion of Catholic teachers (since they belong to teaching Orders) have been trained in the Republic and in a somewhat different tradition. Thus out of forty-three teachers at St. Mary's Christian Brothers School in Belfast, only two hold Northern Ireland qualifications.

The mixing which is so carefully prevented at school (even on the games field: see p. 148) occurs with much more freedom in all forms of further or higher education, except teacher training. Thus the school (Stanhope Street Further Education Centre) run by the Belfast education authority for young people on day release is mixed; the technical colleges (a growing field of education) are mixed; the Belfast Domestic Science Training College has about 20 per cent of Catholics among its students; adult education classes organized by the Joint Committee of the University and the Workers' Educational Association are not normally divided according to religion. But at the end of 1960 there were two Catholic students among the 995 teachers in training at Stranmillis Training College, and there were no Protestants among the 509 students (in 1959-60) at St. Mary's Training College.

The great example of mixed higher education is provided by the Queen's University of Belfast. This was one of the three Queen's Colleges founded in 1845 at Belfast, Cork, and Galway, under an Act which prohibited all preference to a particular religion. In practice Belfast was during its early years mainly attended by Presbyterians (members of the Church of Ireland tending to go to Trinity College, Dublin), while Cork and Galway attracted some Catholics. The principle of non-discrimination, however, survived, and was continued when (by the Irish Universities Act of 1908) the Belfast College became a separate University. Thus religious ministrations are committed to Deans of Residences appointed by the various churches, and the University gives them help only to find the students which belong to their flock; there is no chapel in the University; the Faculty of Theology is an appendage, not paid for out of University funds, to provide facilities for the Presbyterian and Methodist Churches; and all

University teachers must sign a declaration that they will not say anything disrespectful to the religious opinions of their students. The nearest approach to the recognition of religious differences is the existence of a department of Scholastic Philosophy, staffed by Catholic scholars, mainly attended by Catholic students, and separate from the teaching of moral philosophy and logic and metaphysics. This department owes its existence to a proposal in April 1909 by five Catholic members of the original or 'charter' senate of the Queen's University. They proposed also a second appointment in history and English literature, an arrangement to bring the Mater Hospital into touch with the University, and the appointment of a professor of Celtic languages and literature; if these recommendations were adopted, they said, 'we have reason to believe that they will induce large numbers of students to become members of the University who otherwise may go elsewhere'.[8]

The establishment of a lectureship in scholastic philosophy aroused much controversy, and was the subject of appeals to the universities committee of the Irish Privy Council. These appeals were dismissed; and, since in addition the Mater Hospital was recognized as a teaching hospital and a lectureship in Celtic was established, a substantial gesture of friendship had been made to the Catholic community, and in consequence they made a much larger use of the University than before. The proportion of Catholic students rose sharply from 5 per cent in 1909 to 25 per cent in 1915; it fell during the inter-war period, but has now returned to about 22 per cent. Given the economic pressure on the Catholic community and the low proportion going to grammar schools, this is about the percentage which one would expect to find. Catholic students are 35 per cent of the total in the Arts Faculty, 30 per cent in Law, but only 17 per cent in Applied Science and 14 per cent in Pure Science (1959–60 figures); these differences follow from the weakness of science teaching in many Catholic grammar schools, and perhaps also from the occupational structure of the Catholic community. Religion is regarded as irrelevant to the selection of teaching staff. Relative to the numbers in the Northern Ireland population, the proportion of Catholics on the University staff is low; this is because, by long tradition (and unlike the Scottish universities), Queen's

8 T. W. Moody and J. C. Beckett, *Queen's, Belfast*, vol. 1, p. 407.

recruits its staff without any local preference (and indeed with some preference for those who have had experience outside Northern Ireland). The effective area of selection is thus the United Kingdom, and the proportion of Catholics on the staff tends to reproduce the proportion in the United Kingdom as a whole, rather than that in Northern Ireland.

Relations between students from the two communities are good, and there is considerable mixing in university societies and clubs. Questions to students have not elicited any strong sense of religious group feeling, though there is no doubt that both the Catholics and the evangelical Protestants are conscious of the general unity of their respective communities.

A special feature in the field of university education is provided by Magee University College at Londonderry. The foundation of Martha Maria Magee was a combination of a liberal arts college and a Presbyterian theological college; but in 1951 the two sides were separated, and the non-theological part of the College was left with the main function of providing the first two years of certain courses for Trinity College, Dublin, or the first year of certain courses for Queen's University. Because of the Presbyterian origins of the College, and the situation of special tension existing in Londonderry, there is little Catholic participation in courses; but it is encouraging that any exists at all.

In what ways will the schooldays of a Protestant separate him from his Catholic neighbours, other than by the removal of opportunities of friendship between schoolfellows? One difference is in the teaching of history. As a broad generalization, the non-Catholic schools teach English history, as being a well-established discipline with good textbooks, which tells children about their own country (which is the United Kingdom). Irish history is therefore taught as an incidental to English history. Catholic schools are more likely to teach Irish history in its own right, and to treat it as the story of heroism in maintaining national feeling under foreign rule. Examination of the Ministry of Education's papers for the Junior and Senior Certificates (the latter roughly corresponding to the General Certificate of Education) shows that, while a knowledge of Irish history might give some help in widening the choice of questions, it would be possible to omit it altogether. The great obstacle to the teaching of Irish history has been the lack of adequate textbooks, particularly at the junior level; if this handicap were overcome, the two communities might move closer to a common practice, since some Catholic teachers feel that a broader treatment of history would help to open children's minds to the importance of the world outside Ireland.

Another difference in the Catholic schools is the teaching of Irish, which is a recognized subject in both Junior and Senior Certificates. This is no doubt valuable as a means of understanding the cultural background of the country (and for this purpose a few Protestants learn it in later life), though there are practically no natural users of Irish in Northern Ireland. But a wider choice of language might give a better use of school time; in practice Irish is often dropped after the Junior Certificate, and its mainte-nance for the earlier years of education owes much to nationalist political sentiment. Most Protestants regard Irish as a largely dead and useless language; some Catholics regard it as an important part of their birthright.

We have had numerous complaints from both sides of derogatory and slanderous teachings about the other group, im-parted in the classroom. These complaints are usually vague; but some are no doubt fully justified, for among ten thousand teachers there are bound to be some irresponsible bigots and fanatics. Protestants have told us that Catholic children are deliberately taught to look on all Protestants as wrong and wicked, and are carefully trained to be anti-British Irish nationalists; but Catholics deny that they teach hatred of Protestants. Catholics have complained to us that Protestants are taught to hate the Catholic faith and to mistrust Catholics as persons; but on the other hand many Protestant teachers claim it to be their duty to encourage tolerance and to try to counteract some of the bigotry which children absorb from their homes. Obviously there is no way of drawing up a fair account; but on balance it is very likely that the teaching profession, composed of educated and reasonable men and women, is an influence against bitterness rather than a stimulant of it. In so far as this is not the case, it is because everyone in Northern Ireland is to some extent caught by the bonds of past history, whose importance in education we have shown in this chapter.

CHAPTER 6

DISCRIMINATION IN EMPLOYMENT

BEFORE we examine the employment opportunities available in Northern Ireland, two preliminary points must be made. The first is that the existence of *some* discrimination on grounds of religion, on the part both of Protestants and of Catholics, is beyond doubt; the interesting question is not the existence of discrimination, but how far it distorts the pattern of employment. The second point is that discrimination cannot always be proved by statistics of the religion of those employed—it may be, for instance, that a deficiency of Catholics in positions of responsibility in some firm is a result of their lower social status and shorter period of education; or is simply due to the segregation of the communities into different areas of housing. One must, if possible, look at policy and not only at results.

We have often been told, both by Protestants and by Catholics, that discrimination in employment is perfectly natural: 'A man should look after his own.' Many members of both communities consider that preference on grounds of religion or politics is obviously right—the Protestants regarding this as the best way of maintaining their supremacy and the all-important safeguards of the constitution: the Catholics considering that, since they suffer most from poverty and unemployment, it is only reasonable that their members should have preference. (A pamphlet issued by the St. George's Ward Unionist Association on the occasion of the 1961 Belfast municipal elections stated that its three candidates 'employ over 70 People, and have NEVER employed A ROMAN CATHOLIC'.)[1] Mr. Robert Babington, speaking to the Unionist Labour Association in Belfast on 4 March 1961, is reported by the *Irish Times* to have said:

'Registers of unemployed loyalists should be kept by the Unionist Party and employers invited to pick employees from them. The Unionist Party should make it quite clear that it is loyalists who have the first

[1] *Sunday Independent* photograph, 21 May 1961.

choice of jobs. There is nothing wrong in this. Indeed, just the reverse; the Unionist Party was founded to further the objects of the loyalists.'

The Minister of Labour and National Insurance, speaking on an adjournment motion occasioned by Mr. Babington's speech, denied that this represented Government policy, in the following words:

'When we as a Ministry through the medium of our employment exchanges are invited to submit workers to employers who are looking for staff, we do so without respect to religion ... There is only one distinct preference exercised by the Government, and that is the preference that is exercised in regard to ex-Service personnel ... Clearly and unmistakably, (it is) the policy of the Government, in so far as we enter into the matter of employment, to give fair play to all without discrimination towards any.'[2]

The political arguments about discrimination are mixed with others which have to do with social class and with the suspicion felt for those who are 'different'. Thus some Protestant employers feel that Catholics are not to be trusted, that they are shifty, idle, and unreliable, and fit only to be employed on unskilled work. Since a great many workers do not manage to rise above the occupational class of their parents, a group which is confined to unskilled labour in one generation will produce many unskilled labourers in the next.

Other employers feel, quite simply, that a man has a right to do what he likes with his own money, and that what employment policy he follows is no business of his neighbours. In this view, it may be unfortunate if the sum-total of the decisions of employers looks like discrimination, but the individual decisions cannot rightly be questioned.

In what follows we have had to keep in mind the danger of maintaining antagonisms by publishing facts about the employment practices of different firms and bodies. Much of the discrimination takes place without any need to turn down qualified applicants—it is generally understood that at A Protestants need not apply, and at B Catholics will be unwelcome. There is sometimes a fear of letting in a single member of the other community (especially to a position of responsibility), on the grounds that

[2] *Hansard*, 7 March 1961, cols. 756, 758.

where one comes others will follow: 'Before you know where you are, the whole place will be full of them.' But we do not wish to perpetuate any practices which may be ready for change, and we have therefore had recourse in appropriate cases both to anonymity and to vague descriptions of firms so that they cannot be recognized.

English readers should remember that in Northern Ireland it is not usually necessary to be so blunt as to ask a man his religion. It is sufficient to ask where he went to school; for (as we have seen in the last chapter) segregation in education is almost complete. Therefore it is possible (for instance) for the Northern Ireland Government to deny any knowledge of the religion of its civil servants, since no question about religion is asked, while at the same time those who interview, appoint, or promote civil servants will be perfectly well aware of which community the man belongs to.

The Civil Service

The Northern Ireland Civil Service, with over 8,000 permanent and temporary staff, consists of Ministries of Finance, Agriculture, Commerce, Education, Health and Local Government, Home Affairs, and Labour and National Insurance, together with various smaller departments and offices, and the Royal Ulster Constabulary. We have not been able to classify all employees, but with the assistance of various past and present members of the service we have obtained a tolerably accurate breakdown by religion of the administrative grades and staff officers in the main departments, both for 1927 and for 1959. The former year is taken as representing the state of the administration when it had settled down after its transfer from Dublin Castle; at that time, it was natural to expect that a high proportion of Protestants in the old Irish Civil Service would choose transfer to the Protestant part of Ireland. But the following table shows that the proportions by religion in the various grades have hardly changed since. We apologize for any inaccuracy which later research may reveal in this table; but perhaps the most significant thing about it is that it is possible to obtain such a classification at all, for it shows that in Northern Ireland a man's religion is a matter of general interest. It is possible that the proportion of Catholics may have been underestimated, but there seems to be no doubt that the senior civil servants are overwhelmingly Protestant. We have heard a rumour in Protestant circles that '*they* are getting in up there', that is to say up in the Government offices in Stormont, which stand on a hill, but there seems little reason for any such belief about the senior grades.

Analysis of Part of Northern Ireland Civil Service, by Grade and Reported Religious Affiliation, 1927 and 1959

	1927			1959		
	Pro-testant	Catholic	% Pro-testant	Pro-testant	Catholic	% Pro-testant
Permanent Secre-taries	5	1	83	7	—	100
Second and Assist-ant Secretaries, etc.	12	1	92	36	2	95
Principals	40	3	93	103	4	96
Deputy and Assistant Principals	66	3	96	199	17	92
Staff Officers	92	6	94	349	23	94
All persons covered	215	14	94	694	46	94

Since about three-quarters of the grammar school and university population of the Province is Protestant, it would be reasonable to expect at least this proportion of Protestants among holders of higher Civil Service posts. Nor is the difference between 75 per cent and 94 per cent necessarily evidence of discrimination. Since a large proportion of Catholics are politically opposed to the existence of Northern Ireland as a separate state, it would not be a matter for surprise if they failed to apply to join its service. In certain departments any applications might well be suspect on reasonable grounds of security. Thus, it is not surprising that the Ministry of Home Affairs (which is responsible for internal security) appears to have employed in 1959 no Catholics in the rank of Principal or higher,[3] though it is perhaps more curious that the same is true of the Ministry of Labour. Reliable evidence of discrimination or of its absence might be obtained by following

[3] The Royal Ulster Constabulary is in principle recruited from both communities, and repeated efforts have been made to keep the force non-political and to recruit more Catholics to it; but it is not surprising that Catholics are unwilling to join a force which is so widely regarded by nationalists as the 'tool of a foreign power'. A parliamentary question on 7 November 1961 produced the information that 12 per cent of the R.U.C. was then Catholic, 37 per cent Church of Ireland, and 40 per cent Presbyterian.

DISCRIMINATION IN EMPLOYMENT

the careers of Catholics who have entered the service, but (although we have had details of some cases of alleged discrimination) we have had no evidence sufficient to enable us to reach a conclusion.

Fewer inhibitions exist about the posts in the 'Imperial' Civil Service—that is to say the jobs (mainly in the Post Office, the Inland Revenue and Customs and Excise Departments, and the Defence Departments) which come directly under the Government in London. We are told that for these posts the proportion of Catholic applicants is high—more than would be expected on a population basis—and that some Catholic schools give special teaching related to the appropriate entrance examinations. Our evidence about the religion of those who actually enter is sketchy, but there is general agreement that the proportion of Catholics employed is high. Thus we have been given estimates of 33 per cent for the Inland Revenue (with some additional evidence which would suggest a higher figure); of 33–40 per cent for the Customs and Excise; and of 50–55 per cent for the Post Office as a whole, and for the chief Belfast telephone exchange. These figures relate to *all* staff, including industrial grades, and there is evidence (from the Post Office) that the proportion of Protestants is higher in senior positions, perhaps because of a reluctance to transfer a Catholic to a job in Northern Ireland where his religion might count against him in the public contacts required by his work. We have received no suggestions of deliberate discrimination in the Imperial Service.

Local Government

In the local government service discrimination is taken for granted, at least outside Belfast. Thus we are told that in Londonderry, with a Unionist Council (though a majority of the population is Catholic: see p. 120), no Catholics are normally employed in senior positions, though some obtain jobs as labourers. In Newry, with a Catholic majority, all the Urban Council's clerical and outdoor staff were said to be Catholic in 1958.[4] The officers of the Council have assured us, however, that for the clerical and skilled posts there is an examination which is open to all, and that

---

[4] Senator J. T. Fisher, *Hansard*, 4 November 1958, col. 575.

the applicants with the highest marks are taken. A recent senior post was filled by an Englishman, and it was only after he had been appointed on his merits that it was found that he was in fact a Catholic. As for the distribution of labouring jobs, we are told that the Catholic proportion among the unemployed is so high that there is an almost irresistible pressure to give labouring jobs to Catholics.

The nationalist case on discrimination in local government is stated in Frank Gallagher, *The Indivisible Island*,[5] pp. 209–11, and (by courtesy of the Deputy Keeper of Printed Books at the National Library of Ireland) we have seen some of the source material for this book. Assuming that Mr. Gallagher, when he says 'nationalist', means 'Catholic', his figures appear to show that 12 per cent of all executive, administrative, and clerical staff in the Northern Ireland local government service is Catholic (about a third of the population proportion); and that higher grades are commonly reserved to Protestants in Protestant controlled areas, including Belfast, whereas employees such as scavengers are often Catholic. We think that these conclusions are broadly correct, though it is odd that the same zealous research was not extended to a nationalist-controlled area like Newry. The fact is that both sides discriminate, and that the overall pattern of discrimination against Catholics exists because most Councils are in Protestant hands.

The following quotations illustrate the controversy which faces local Councils in ensuring that their supporters get the jobs:

'They saw a lot of people going to the War Memorial on the 11th November to pay tribute to the dead, and now they had a chance to give a man who had come through the war a job, said Mr. Charles McKeown (Anti-Partition) at Fermanagh Education Committee when he proposed the appointment of [X] as caretaker of Enniskillen Technical School. . . . The Technical School Committee had recommended the appointment of [Y] who is not an ex-serviceman. Mr. George Elliot (Unionist) said that [Y] had been temporarily in the job and had been very satisfactory. They had tried three ex-servicemen and an ex policeman and the four of them had let them down. . . . By a strictly party vote of 8 Unionists to 4 Anti-Partitionists [Y] was appointed and the ex-serviceman candidate rejected. [X] is a Catholic and [Y] a

[5] Gollancz, 1957.

Protestant. The four previously appointed who, according to Mr. Elliott, had let the Committee down, were all Protestants.'

(*Irish News*, 5 December 1949.)

'Prior to the appointment of [a man to a senior post under the Newry Council] a resolution was passed that an ex-serviceman should have preference. A local ex-serviceman with very high qualifications applied, but the Catholic and Nationalist members of the Council voted for, and appointed, a man who was not an ex-serviceman, but who was a Catholic.'

(Senator Joseph Fisher, reported in the *Belfast Telegraph*, 4 November 1958.)

'A suggestion that a notice reading "*No Catholic need apply*" be posted on the City Hall door was made . . . at a special meeting of Armagh City Council called to appoint a clerk typist in the Town Clerk's office.'

(*Irish News*, 17 September 1949.)

'A Unionist member left the meeting (of the Board of Daisy Hill Hospital, Newry) in protest, suggesting that the Board should insert a notice "*No Protestant need apply*".'

(Senator Fisher, *Hansard*, 4 November 1958, col. 576.)

We think that the situation which exists in local government will be more readily understood by American than by British readers. Many local councillors take it for granted that they are dispensers of patronage to their own side; and the exercise of this patronage is made easier by the custom of expecting personal canvassing of the Council or of its committee before appointments are made. Some public bodies have managed to stop canvassing, but it is still widely regarded as a proper way to make sure that an applicant has the right personal qualities to fit into a local community.

There was a debate on discrimination in local government in the Northern Ireland House of Commons on 25 April 1961. In general this followed the expected lines, Nationalist members making numerous charges of discrimination by Unionist local authorities, and Unionists defending the freedom of local authorities to do what they like. A Unionist member pointed out the enormous disparity in size between Belfast, with 1,050 clerical staff, and the smaller authorities. 'In Warrenpoint there is a clerk and one girl, in Ballycastle a clerk and two girls, in Keady a clerk only and in Tanderagee a clerk and one assistant who collects the rates and does a whole variety of local council jobs.'[6] It is certainly true that it is not easy to reconcile impartial selection by a competitive examination with the independent status of these very small local authorities.

Private Firms

Our inquiries reveal four different policies, those of:

(a) firms which only employ members of one community;

(b) Protestant-owned firms which employ Catholics only in lower-paid jobs, and not in any administrative or supervisory capacity;

(c) firms employing both Protestants and Catholics, but segregating them by departments;

(d) firms which mix members of the two communities within the same department.

We will illustrate these in turn.

(a) Complete Discrimination

This is the natural pattern in many very small enterprises; if you own a greengrocer's shop, and want an errand-boy, it is natural to look first among your neighbours and friends—and, in the social situation which exists in Ulster, these are likely to be of your own religion. If you want a shop assistant, the preference for someone of your own religion will be reinforced, since a small shop might well lose custom if it were known to employ one of 'the other side'. We have ourselves heard the muttered remark 'Why does Mr. X favour them ones; I don't think he should do a thing like thon.'

A larger business, especially in Belfast (where religious divisions matter less for some purposes), might find it a positive advantage to employ members of both communities, in order to attract customers from both. But this will be offset by the fear of trouble which would impede business or production—trouble which might arise (for instance) from some incident about the flying of the Union Jack, or from some resentful remark about a shooting on the Border. A firm which has grown from small origins and

[6] Mr. Kirk, *Hansard*, 25 April 1961, col. 1424.

which has never employed a member of the other community will find it particularly difficult to venture into the unknown and begin the process of mixing Protestants and Catholics. We have often heard from managers the remark: 'Of course, we wouldn't mind having a Catholic in the office (or the factory); but the workers would never stand for it.' Such an attitude illustrates the tendency of some intelligent people to be slightly ashamed of discrimination, and to wish to shift the responsibility elsewhere. The same unwillingness to admit the practice is shown by the advertisements in newspapers, which no longer state the religion required of applicants for jobs as often as they did in the past.

Here are some examples of complete discrimination:

1. Large food firm employing only Protestants.
2. Two food firms employing only Catholics (except that one has a Protestant manager).
3. Medium-sized engineering firm employing only Protestants: 'We have never had a Catholic, and we do not know how he would get on with the other workers.'
4. Large garage—same attitude.
5. Wholesale food business employing only Catholics.
6. Two printers employing only Protestants because of a fear of losing trade from Protestant customers.
7. Textile firm which took over three Catholic technicians from a works which was closing down, but was forced to dismiss them by a threat of strike action from the other employees.

b) Catholics Only in Lower-Paid Posts

This pattern of behaviour can be produced in several ways. First, some Protestant employers who would prefer to employ only Protestants find that, in a particular area, no one is willing to do lowly-paid, heavy, or dirty work. Second, some employers who are prepared in principle to employ people from both communities hold the belief that Protestants will not work well under Catholic supervision (whereas Catholics can be expected to work under Protestant supervision). This is analogous to the belief which often causes women to be denied senior posts—that men will not work under them. The belief implies a set pattern of superiority and inferiority, known and accepted by both the superior and the inferior party. It is easy to see how a long period of Protestant economic dominance can produce such an attitude.

Some employers have doubts about the employment of Catholics in senior positions because of their nationalist sympathies, similar to the doubts which an English employer might feel about hiring a Communist as a manager. These doubts merge into others which are a consequence of the general fear of the strange and the unknown. For instance, it is held that Catholics cannot be trusted with business secrets because they will tell them all to the priest; that they will gossip to members of their own community about the firm's business; that they have no regard for truth, especially when dealing with Protestants, whom they regard as heretics. There is also a belief, which perhaps has more substance, that a Catholic in a responsible position will 'pack' the firm with other Catholics; no doubt this tendency operates also for Protestants.

The following are examples of this form of partial discrimination:

1. Textile firm: 30 per cent of employees Catholic (above local population proportion), but only one foreman and no one in an executive position.

2. Wholesale merchants: no Catholics on salaried staff because the Managing Director has what he admits to be an irrational distrust of them: half of wage-earners Catholic (above local population proportion).

3. Clothing firm: 90 per cent of women workers Catholic, but none in the office or in an administrative capacity.

4. Engineering firm: Protestant personnel officer, chief executives English, supervisory personnel Protestant (except for an inspector and two foremen, out of sixteen); but Catholics are employed on the shop floor.

5. Merchants and importers: 50 per cent Catholic labour, but none in the office—'You can't work with Catholics in executive positions.' The difficulty in this case seems to have been nationalist politics.

6. Firm in food industry, Catholic-owned and employing mainly Catholics, but uses Protestants on its office staff.

(c) Segregation by Departments

This type of arrangement may occur either by a decision of an employer, that he will not discriminate but that segregation will avoid trouble, or by natural growth, a Protestant departmental head appointing Protestants and a Catholic appointing Catholics. The second tendency is frequently feared, and we have no doubt that it often occurs. In an area of general unemployment,[7] it is often easy to recruit labour from one's own friends, and there is little reason to extend one's inquiries farther afield. A special case of segregation is to be found in the docks—the cross-Channel traffic is handled by members of the Amalgamated Transport and General Workers' Union, who are mostly Protestant, while the 'deep sea' traffic is handled by members of the Irish Transport and General Workers' Union, who are almost all Catholic. Other examples of segregation by departments are:

1. Textile firm: workers Protestant, there being a Protestant foreman: office staff Catholic, the office supervisor being of that religion.
2. Textile firm: spinning shed Protestant and weaving shed Catholic.

(d) Mixing within Departments and at all or most Grades

'Mixed' firms are often controlled by interests outside Northern Ireland, and have English or Scottish managers who take no great interest (at first) in the religion of their employees, except to stamp out extreme expressions of nationalism or bigotry which may endanger productive efficiency. There are of course some Northern Ireland managers who on principle do not discriminate, and large firms are often scrupulously impartial in their employment policy. It must be remembered, however, that the principle of 'the best man for the job' will often give a large proportion of Protestants at the higher levels, simply because the advancement of Catholics is hampered by low social status. As far as we have been able to discover, public boards and nationalized industries follow the employment policy here described.

[7] Since the war, the unemployment rate in Ulster has varied between 5 per cent and 12 per cent; a rate of 10·9 per cent (12·5 per cent for men) was reached in April 1958. Unemployment of unskilled workers is widespread throughout the country.

Here are some examples from private firms:

1. Large engineering firm, with English connexions, probably employing almost 50 per cent Catholics (including some in senior managerial posts), but with a deficiency of Catholic foremen. This firm uses modern methods of personnel selection and promotion, and the procedure gives little opportunity for discrimination.

2. Processor of agricultural material, with foreign connexions. This firm has had to take strong action to stop quarrels (e.g. dismissing an employee for writing up an anti-Catholic slogan); mixing takes place at all levels. Recruitment is controlled by an Englishman.

3. Food industry firm, with English connexions: executive and office staff mostly Protestant, foremen mostly Catholic, workers 85 per cent Catholic (but the factory is in a Catholic area). This firms tries to give equal importance to Catholic and Protestant holidays.

4. Engineering firm, with English connexions: about 35 per cent Catholics, though the factory is in a Protestant area; rather more Catholics at junior supervisory levels, and fewer at senior levels. All recruitment is done by the Personnel Manager, who seems to be strictly impartial. There has been a little trouble due to attempts to 'pack' departments with members of one community.

5. Food industry firm, owned by an Ulster Protestant, in a Catholic area. This firm shows a remarkable degree of mixing at all levels (the Managing Director is Catholic): about 70 per cent of all workers are Catholic, but with some Protestants in all departments.

6. Textile firm, Ulster ownership: as a matter of principle this firm does not discriminate, but it has to be careful to restrict provocative actions, e.g. around the 12th of July.

We have considered whether it would be possible to find some direct statistical measure of the results of the practices described in this chapter, but we have concluded that it would be impossible to do this. Apart from the difficulty of persuading a representative sample of employers to answer questions, we should undoubtedly find that many of the larger employers have no reliable statistics about the effect of their own employment practices, and that it would be necessary to repeat (on a much larger scale and on much more difficult material) the exercise which we undertook for a part of the Northern Ireland Civil Service.

There is no doubt that Protestant dominance in the business executive and professional life of the Province goes much beyond what would be indicated by the proportion of the population belonging to that community; so that, if Protestant and Catholic employers on average discriminate to the same extent, the job opportunities for Catholics will be below average and those for Protestants above average. In addition, there is a deficiency of jobs for unskilled labourers, and the lower social status of Catholics would therefore be reflected in a higher unemployment rate. But, although it is generally believed (and is indeed certain) that the ranks of the unemployed contain an undue proportion of Catholics, there is no direct measure of this, since the unemployed are not classified by religion.

It is, however, possible to get some measure of the problem by examining the estimates of unemployment percentages for local areas, which have recently been made available by the Ministry of Labour. On 10 July 1961 the local employment exchange areas with the highest proportions of unemployed were:

Newry	17·2 per cent unemployed
Newcastle	16·4
Strabane	14·4
Londonderry	13·8
Limavady	13·0
Ballymoney	11·7

while the lowest proportions were found in:

Ballyclare	2·2
Bangor	2·7
Lisburn	3·3
Carrickfergus	3·5
Newtownards	4·2
Ballynahinch	4·6
Ballymena	4·9
Belfast	5·6

The Northern Ireland proportion at that time was 7·0 per cent. The concentration of unemployment on the Border towns is most marked, and these are towns which mostly have a Catholic majority. In contrast, the towns which surround Belfast, with Protestant majorities, are with a few exceptions places of relatively low unemployment.

In the House of Commons on 3 May 1961, the Minister of Labour was asked by Mr. Diamond how many unemployed juveniles in Belfast were educated at Catholic voluntary schools. The following exchange took place:

'*The Minister of Labour and National Insurance (Major Neill)*: On 10th April, 1961, there were 195 juveniles on the unemployed register in Belfast. Statistics about the schools at which these juveniles were educated are not maintained by the Ministry.

'I am informed that officers of the Youth Advisory Service give advice to the majority of young persons about to leave school in the Belfast area. By arrangement with the education authority any juveniles who come on the unemployed register are seen by these officers, so that all unemployed juveniles in Belfast receive guidance from the service.

'During the past 12 months 2,046 vacancies for juveniles were filled by the Ministry's employment office in Belfast. The placing statistics do not show the schools which the juveniles had attended.

'*Mr. Diamond:* Is the Minister aware that sources connected with the Catholic voluntary schools reveal that something like 70 per cent of those who are utilizing this service come from those schools? Does he not recognize that this shows there is a marked degree of sectarian discrimination in the allocation of employment to juveniles? . . .

'*Major Neill:* I rise only to emphasize what I have said on many occasions to the hon. Member for Falls (Mr. Diamond)—that as far as my Ministry is concerned I refute entirely his charges of discrimination on grounds of religion in the placing of any of our people, whether they be juveniles or adults, in employment.'[8]

It appears to us that because of the way in which the Youth Advisory Service is organized, the approximate proportion of Catholics among the juvenile unemployed must certainly be known, though we accept the fact that it is not recorded among the Ministry of Labour's statistics. We think it likely that the proportion is high, and may be as high as 70 per cent; but it will

[8] *Hansard*, 3 May 1961, cols. 1688–9.

be noted that the numbers involved are quite small. Employers can, of course, discriminate if they wish, and we should be surprised if the officers of the Ministry and of the Youth Advisory Service fail to maintain unofficial lists, showing employers to whom Protestants or Catholics (as the case may be) need not apply.

But perhaps the most striking measure of the difference in economic opportunity is to be found in the emigration rate. The calculations which follow relate to the periods 1937–51 and 1951–61.

In 1951 there were in the Province 368,000 children born since 1937. The total number of births over the period was 402,000, the difference representing children who have died, together with the net effect of the emigration or immigration of children with their parents. Of the 368,000 children in 1951, 40·8 per cent were Catholic; assuming that at least as high a proportion of the losses over the period 1937–51 were Catholic, it would appear that Catholic births were 164,000. There is no sufficient evidence of a higher Catholic death rate (though it may be a little higher); let us assume that deaths of members of the various denominations, over the period, were divided in the population proportion for 1937. On this reckoning 82,000 Catholics died between 1937 and 1951, and if we assume (as is reasonable) that there is no considerable net loss by conversions we have:

Catholic Numbers, 1937 . . .	428,000
+ Births	164,000
− Deaths	82,000
Expected Number, 1951, if there were no emigration	510,000
Catholic Numbers, 1951 . . .	471,000
Emigration .	39,000

The corresponding figures for the second period are:

Catholic Numbers, 1951 . . .	471,000
+ Births	130,000
− Deaths	52,000
Expected Number, 1961, if there were no emigration	549,000
Catholic Numbers, 1961 . . .	498,000
Emigration .	51,000

Repeating this calculation for other denominations, we have:

Apparent Emigration by Denomination

				1937–51	1951–61
Catholic	.	.	.	39,000	51,00
All Protestant	.	.	.	28,000	41,00
Presbyterian	.	18,000		25,000	
Church of Ireland	.	17,000		34,000	
Methodist	.	.	−4,000	} −18,000	
Others	.	.	−3,000		
Total	.	.	.	67,000	92,00

The figures for individual Protestant denominations aré un realistic, since there is a significant movement between them b conversion, which has been ignored. The table shows that th Catholic one-third of the population gave rise to 55–58 per cen of the emigration. Relating the emigrants to the numbers at th beginning of the period, we have:

Effects of Emigration or Conversion, 1937–51 and 1951–61, as a Percentage of Numbers in 1937 and 1951

					1937–51	1951–61
Catholic	.	.	.	.	9% loss	9% loss
Protestant	.	.	.	.	3% loss	4% loss
Presbyterian	.	.	.		5% loss	6% loss
Church of Ireland	.	.	.		5% loss	8% loss
Methodist	.	.	.		7% gain }	13% gain
Others	.	.	.	.	6% gain }	

These calculations are interesting not only as a rough measur of the difference in the economic opportunities available at hom to members of the two communities. They suggest that emigratio is just about sufficient to drain off the excess births in the Catholi community, and keep the proportions of Protestants and Catholic almost stable; they are in fact still very close to the levels at whicl they stood at the foundation of the state forty years ago. Thu the difference in economic opportunity is a regulator maintainin the *status quo*.

CHAPTER 7

SOME FEATURES
OF THE SOCIAL SERVICES

THE statutory social services of Northern Ireland are for the most part copied from those of Great Britain, though with some local differences in administration. Thus the system of National Insurance contributions and benefits is the same as in Britain; the money received from contributions is paid into separate Northern Ireland funds, but there is a financial adjustment with the British funds so that National Insurance operates as a single system throughout the United Kingdom. Under the Social Services (Agreement) Act (N.I.), 1949, the Northern Ireland Exchequer also receives payments from the Imperial Government designed to equalize the burdens of national assistance, old age pensions, family allowances, and the health services. These payments are of the order of £5 million a year, and it is clearly much easier to justify them if the services to which they relate are identical on the two sides of the Irish Sea. Furthermore, it is strongly held by those who support the present constitution that the citizens of Northern Ireland are entitled as of right to any benefits provided in the rest of the United Kingdom.

The policy of copying Britain, known as the 'step by step' policy, thus meant that in the immediate post-war years the Unionist Government at Stormont was recommending to Parliament measures which had been passed by a Labour Government at Westminster against Conservative opposition. There was political benefit in such a course, for the advantages of the Welfare State have remained ever since a good propaganda point to use against those who desire union with the Republic. However, the post-war reforms were quite genuinely welcomed for their own sake by many Unionists, for the broad scope of the Unionist Party finds room for a radical and reforming outlook.

It is a necessary consequence of the 'step by step' policy that the Northern Ireland statutory social services in general take no account of religion in their administration (since no account is taken of it in Britain). In practice the social services operate so as to help the Catholic community more than the Protestant; there are relatively more poor Catholics (and therefore more National Assistance payments), more unemployed Catholics (and therefore more unemployment benefit), and bigger Catholic families (and therefore more family allowances). The Family Allowances Acts, since they offer help to the second and subsequent children, are particularly effective in helping big families; the allowance for a family of six children is not three but six times as large as the allowance for a family of two. Family allowances were in 1956 the subject of an unsuccessful attempt to depart from the 'step by step' policy. In that year the Imperial Government increased allowances in Britain, formerly 8s. a week for the second and subsequent children, to 8s. for the second child and 10s. for the subsequent children. The Northern Ireland Minister of Labour and National Insurance, Major Neill, proposed to introduce allowances (of similar total cost) of 9s. 6d. for the second and third child and 8s. thereafter. Speaking on the second reading of his Bill on 6 June 1956, he said :

'Family allowances are not required here with a view to bringing about any increase in our population. Such an increase could only make our position more difficult to solve and create greater problems for the future. As it is, the high rates of insurance have been a major cause of the chronic under-employment which has for so long been a feature of our economy. In these circumstances the proper aim of a family allowance scheme in Northern Ireland should be to increase the standard of living for as many of our families as possible.'[1]

His proposals would have benefited 104,000 families, whereas the British scheme, if adopted, would only have benefited 57,000.

The Minister's proposals were strongly criticized (notably by the *Belfast Telegraph*). Many Unionists were doubtful about the wisdom of risking the benefits of the 'step by step' policy by this particular measure. Social workers were indignant about a proposal which seemed to amount to controlling population by means of poverty—at the cost of hardship for the existing children in large families. Not only Catholics but many others regarded the measure as intended to discriminate against the minority. The General

[1] *Hansard*, 6 June 1956, col. 1788.

ssembly of the Presbyterian Church, while not asserting that the
roposals were intended to hurt the Catholics, passed the following
solution:

'In as much as the reduction in family allowances has been interpreted
ɣ a section of the community as an intentional and political discrimina-
ɔn against them, and may be so interpreted by others outside Northern
eland, the Assembly urges the Government to bring their proposed
gislation on this matter into line with that of the Imperial Govern-
ent.'[2]

n 12 June the Prime Minister announced that, in view of the
ıblic comment, the Government would introduce an amendment
the committee stage of the Bill to preserve uniformity with Great
ritain.

We have heard no recent complaints of discrimination in the
lministration of those welfare services which give cash benefits
pensions.[3] Complaints are indeed made, of a different kind: that
zy and good-for-nothing Catholics live in comfortable idleness
ι the benefits of the Welfare State, and that people fraudulently
aim unemployment benefit when they are working. The facts on
ese matters are difficult to establish. No one, of course, can attain
uch comfort on State benefits, but it is probably true that these
enefits can provide a standard of living which compares favour-
ɔly with the pre-war poverty in parts of the Ulster countryside.
he authorities naturally take steps to protect the insurance and
sistance funds against fraud, but this protection cannot be ab-
lute without having inquiries which would be intolerably burden-
me to those in genuine need. But the feeling voiced by some
rotestants that Catholics, with the advice of their Church, are
cessively assiduous in claiming their rights to benefit, and indulge
underhand practices to get more, probably owes much to resent-
ent at those who 'bite the hand which feeds them'. The kind of
mark which we have heard is: 'They abuse our State and yet
t every penny they can out of it; if they love the Republic so
uch, why don't they go and live there—and see what they would
t then.' Colour is given to Protestant accusations by the advice

---

[2] *Belfast News-Letter*, 12 June 1956.
[3] Two cases of refusal by local authorities of scholarships to well-qualified
ıdents were quoted to us, though they occurred some time ago. In each case
was necessary to appeal to the Ministry of Education to obtain redress.

given in a pamphlet by a Nationalist member of Parliament, to g
as much out of the State as possible and then 'act stupid, deman
explanations, object, anything at all that will clog the Department
machinery'.[4] But this attitude is, as we know, deplored by man
Catholics, and we have heard many tributes to the benefits receive
from the Welfare State.

Since education has already been discussed in Chapter 5, th
most important State social services which require consideratio
other than those providing cash benefits, are those relating
housing and health. Very few houses were built in Northern Ir
land between the two world wars, and in 1945 there was a larg
unsatisfied need, both to relieve overcrowding and to impro
standards. Since then almost 100,000 dwellings have been pr
vided, about a quarter by the Northern Ireland Housing Trust an
the rest in equal proportions by local authorities and on priva
account. Building by private persons has been encouraged by
capital subsidy on houses below a certain size; this has proved
valuable means of stimulating building at modest cost to th
Exchequer.

The Northern Ireland Housing Trust is a State-appointed, b
autonomous, public authority, financed by Government loans an
assisted by subsidies, and responsible to the Minister for Healt
and Local Government. It has a world-wide reputation for th
provision of well planned and competently administered housir
estates. It selects its tenants both from direct applications and fro
the local authority waiting lists, using a strict points system
determine priority. We understand that the Housing Trust,
addition to rejecting applicants who are well enough off to provic
their own housing, will not accept applicants whose income is s
low that the high rents of post-war property would be an unreasor
able burden. Such a rule would bear more hardly on Catholics tha
Protestants, but it cannot be considered as 'discrimination' unle
one believes that the provision of house-room should have n
relation to ability to pay. We have heard many tributes to the fai
ness and just dealing of the Housing Trust with members of bot
communities, and virtually no complaints; it is clear that the Tru
does provide substantially for Catholics as well as Protestants, an

[4] *Irish Action*, by E. McAteer (published by the *Donegal Democrat*, Ball
shannon, 1948).

n some cases (e.g. Londonderry) helps to relieve an otherwise
desperate shortage of housing for Catholics.

As might be expected, however,[5] there are many complaints of
discrimination by local authorities. The following are examples of
these complaints:

(a) 40 houses at Coneywarren, Co. Tyrone, allocated by Omagh
Rural Council to 'Tories' (i.e. Unionists), 'a majority of
whom were either not married at all or were married and
without children or had but one child', the alleged purpose
being to increase the Unionist vote in North Tyrone (1950).

(b) 70 houses at Dungannon: 'the Unionist majority on the
Council decided that not one was to go to a Catholic' (1958).

(c) 497 houses built at Newry: 'there are at the moment 480
occupied by Nationalists' (1958).

(d) 250 houses built by Strabane Urban District Council: 'of
that total 231 are occupied by Nationalists' (1958).

(e) In Enniskillen 'we have the spectacle of a whole housing
estate where Nationalists cannot put in their nose. The applicants for any of the 95 houses in Derrychara must be of the
right colour' (1958). But this is countered by the statement
that in Enniskillen at least 40 per cent of the Council *and*
Housing Trust houses were occupied by Catholics, and that
when the Council had carried out its slum clearance scheme
there would be more Catholics as tenants than Protestants
(1959). (The Catholic proportion of the population in 1951
was 56 per cent, probably implying a smaller proportion of
families.)

(f) Downpatrick: 'a proportion of two to one in favour of
Nationalists', but 'only 10 per cent of the houses were allocated to Unionists' (1958).[6]

[5] See p. 97 above.

[6] (a) *Discrimination* (All-Party Anti-Partition Conference, 1951). This pamph-
et also quotes, from a 1944 report on housing, figures of the large housing needs
f Londonderry, of Counties Fermanagh and Tyrone, and of the main areas of
Catholic residence in Belfast; but this is evidence of poverty rather than of
discrimination. (b) *Hansard*, 2 April 1958, col. 61 (Mr. J. Stewart). (c), (d)
Hansard, 20 May 1958, col. 883 (Mr. H. W. West). (e) *Hansard*, 20 May 1958,
ol. 865 (Mr. Cahir Healy) and *Belfast News-Letter*, 8 September 1959 (the
Mayor of Enniskillen). (f) *Hansard*, 25 November 1958, col. 877 (Mr. W. B.
Faulkner).

On the other hand, Londonderry claims that it has built twice as many houses for Catholic tenants as for Protestants; but this includes houses built by the Housing Trust, on whose Creggan estate it proved to be possible to allocate only about a dozen houses to Protestants, out of over 1,000 built up to 1958. (The number of houses built at Creggan by the Housing Trust up to 1961 was 1,231.)

Some Councils (including Belfast and Newry) use a points system for allocating houses. In other areas, where canvassing is an accepted practice, and councillors regard it as natural that they should care for their own people, it is hardly surprising that complaints of discrimination should be made.

The health services of Northern Ireland, though somewhat different in their structure, are similar in effect to the services in Britain, and they provide for the needs of the population without discrimination. Sectarian trouble in this field has been confined to one issue—the status of the Mater Infirmorum Hospital in Belfast. This is a Catholic hospital of about 200 beds, recognized as a teaching hospital by Queen's University (and thus used by Catholic medical students for clinical training), and recognized by the General Nursing Council for the training of nurses.

The Bill presented in the autumn of 1947 to establish a National Health Service in Northern Ireland appeared at first to propose the vesting of *all* hospitals in a single Hospitals Authority. This caused difficulty with the voluntary hospitals in general, and the Minister had to make a number of concessions to the views expressed. But the problem of the Mater Hospital was of a different kind; it was argued that this hospital, served by nursing Sisters and with its own chapel, was essentially part of the ministry of healing of the Catholic Church, and could not be placed under a wholly secular control. The National Health Service Acts for England and Wales (1946) and for Scotland (1947) provide that 'where the character and associations of any voluntary hospital transferred to the Minister by virtue of this Act are such as to link it with a particular religious denomination, regard shall be had in the general administration of the hospital and in the making of appointments to the Hospital Management Committee to the preservation of the character and associations of the hospital' (s. 61 of the 1946 Act). The Northern Ireland Bill, in clause 23(4), provided that 'the Authority should so far as is practicable secure that the

objects for which any property transferred to them was used imme-
diately before the appointed day are not prejudiced by reason of
the transfer'. Other clauses (28(7), 29(7)) provided for the continuation of management committees and for the preservation of
the character and associations of the hospitals. The Minister of
Health therefore considered that his Bill provided the same protection as the British Act, and was in fact 'more specific, more
detailed and more direct'.[7]

Even under the British Acts, however, some 200 voluntary hospitals have remained outside the National Health Service, having
requested the Minister to 'disclaim' them as unnecessary to the
adequacy of the service in their particular region, and it is not
likely that the adoption of the British wording would have satisfied
Catholic objections; for to say what the Minister shall 'have regard
to' is not to say precisely what he must do. Mrs. Irene Calvert
proposed that, instead of vesting the hospital in the Hospitals
Authority, it should remain under Church ownership and be leased
to the Authority.[8] The Minister, however, would not accept this
proposal, nor any amendment which would treat one hospital dif-
ferently from the rest. An amendment moved by Dr. MacSorley
proposed a scheme of exemption which the Minister described as
putting the hospital 'half in and half out'; he was prepared to go
'step by step' with Britain, and indeed to go farther (by vesting the
hospitals in an independent body and not in the State as such), but
he would not make more concessions.

In Great Britain Regional Hospital Boards have on occasion
made contractual arrangements with independent hospitals for the
treatment of patients, especially convalescent cases, and payment
has been made from public funds. One possibility, therefore,
(though not a very satisfactory one) would have been for the Hospitals Authority to pay for patients at the Mater Hospital in so far
as that hospital was providing a service which could not be provided
in the Authority's own hospitals—in fact, to use the Mater Hospital as an overflow.[9] But against this it could be argued that independent hospitals in Britain had been 'disclaimed' *by decision of the*

[7] *Hansard*, 9 October 1947, col. 1771.

[8] *Hansard*, 9 October 1947, col. 1748: see also col. 1779.

[9] A proposal of this kind was made by the Tanner Committee (*Report of the
Committee on the Health Services in Northern Ireland*, Cmd. 334, 1955).

Minister, and that in making payments he was in effect partially reversing his disclaimer; whereas the Mater Hospital[10] was staying out *by its own choice*, and had no rights or reasonable claim against public funds.

We have found that many Protestants, as well as Catholics, regard this as a narrow and legalistic argument, and would like to see the State give some aid to the Mater Hospital.[11] There is an excuse for treating it as a special case, for it is the only Roman Catholic teaching hospital in the United Kingdom. The consequences of staying out have been not only to leave the cost of maintenance, drugs, dressings, etc., to be met by voluntary funds, but also to deny to the staff consultant appointments under the National Health Service.

In the direction of the statutory social services, voluntary effort still plays an important part in the work of a variety of committees. Complaint is made that the Catholic community is under-represented on these committees; the following statistics illustrate the point:[12]

	Number of Members	Approximate Proportion of Catholics
General Health Services Board	24	8%
Hospitals Authority	24	8%
31 Local Hospital Management Committees	478	12%

The low proportion of Catholics might in theory lead to discrimination in the making of appointments by the committees. An accusation of this kind against the Hospitals Authority was made in the Northern Ireland Senate on 21 June 1960 by Dr. J. P. Donaghy; but another Catholic, Senator John A. McGlade, replied:

'I as a member of the Hospitals Authority could not agree that the members of that Authority indulge in bigotry or sectarianism in any way.

[10] A second hospital, the U.V.F. Hospital, also remained independent. It should be noted, however, that the Daisy Hill Hospital in Newry is under the Hospitals Authority although it is staffed by nurses from a Catholic Order.

[11] See *Ulster Labour and the Sixties*, issued by the Northern Ireland Labour Party, 1962, p. 12.

[12] See also a paper by Rev. M. P. Kelly, Dean of Residences, the Queen's University, released to the press 3 December 1961.

I have been on practically every committee of that Authority and during many years of membership I can truthfully say that I have never seen any evidence of any bias on the part of any single member. . . . I have had the experience on two or three occasions of Catholic employees of the Authority getting into trouble and appealing their case to the Authority. I would be guilty of the basest inconsideration and treachery if I did not say here and now that I was tremendously impressed with the efforts that were made to exonerate these people and give them justice in the fullest possible way.'[13]

The under-representation of Catholics on statutory committees has a number of possible causes. There will be some who feel a hesitation about taking service under a government of whose very existence they disapprove, however good the work involved; while others will feel doubtful about serving on a body where they will not know other people, and may become a conspicuous minority. Those who issue invitations will find it hard to call to mind suitable Catholics, simply because so few have served in the past; it is easier to use the Protestants they know. It can be argued that, though the minority should be represented, there is no reason why it should be represented in proportion to its population, and in consequence no real efforts are made to choose more than one or two Catholics (just as, on so many bodies, one or two women are considered an adequate representation of their sex). The situation is not likely to change except by a deliberate exercise of a new policy.

The voluntary social services of the Province are vigorous, and organized by a great variety of bodies. Some of these have a direct connexion with a particular church; for instance, the Nazareth Lodge Home for Boys (Catholic), the Church of Ireland Mission to the Adult Deaf and Dumb, the Presbyterian Old Age Fund, and the Methodist Orphan Society. Many others have arisen from a direct religious concern. The major social service bodies tend on the whole to draw their strength from the Protestant community, and though they usually welcome Catholic participation if it can be obtained, this participation is sparse and may involve repeated appearances by the same individual on several bodies. The following statistics illustrate the point:

[13] *Hansard* (Senate), 21 June 1960, col. 374.

	Number of Members	Approximate Proportion of Catholics
Northern Ireland Council of Social Service—Council[14]	79	4%
—Executive Committee	24	12%
—All Other Sub-Committees (together)[15]	174	11%
Belfast Council of Social Welfare —Executive Committee	26	4%
—All Other Sub-Committees (together)[15]	98	10%

There is some reason to think that Catholic co-operation in voluntary social service would be increased if Protestants were more ready to seek Catholic help; it is all too easy to keep to the familiar names in one's own community. But it can also be argued that, among the many calls which the Catholic Church makes on its members' time, voluntary social service takes too low a place. Mr. G. B. Newe argued in this way when speaking to the Catholic Social Study Conference at Garron Tower on 4 August 1958:

'There is still need, for example, for the Society of St. Vincent de Paul, in many ways the most notable, the most valuable, the most inspiring of Catholic voluntary organizations. Indeed, as a professional social worker, I welcome this opportunity of paying tribute to the great work done by this Society in many difficult situations, when statutory assistance could not be provided.... We have, too, the Legion of Mary, whose social work in the larger centres of population is of a high quality —unpretentious and practical. Outside these two organizations, and apart from the great work done by the various Orders on behalf of the aged, the infirm and the neglected, we are singularly lacking in voluntary effort, either of a kind purely Catholic in character, or in our co-operation in the very many fields of voluntary service in which our fellow non-Catholic citizens are so active. Indeed, in the field of voluntary social service we have much to learn from our fellow citizens.'

Mr. Newe went on to refer to lack of lay Catholic effort for old people and in youth clubs; to the difficulty of getting Catholics to

[14] The Secretary and the Vice-Chairman are Catholics.
[15] Some double-counting of the same individual on several committees.

serve on committees, and to the fact that many of those who agree to serve rarely attend meetings.

For our present selective purpose, there is no need to examine the voluntary social services in detail. They are not a point of conflict; with initiative on both sides they could become a more valuable area of co-operation. An ex-Moderator of the Presbyterian General Assembly, Dr. Fulton, gave a lead when, in June 1961, he quoted some words of Sir Thomas Taylor: 'We ought, therefore, as far as we can, to draw closer to Roman Catholics in Christian Charity, seeking wherever we may to find ways of co-operation with them in Christian service to our fellow men.'

CHAPTER 8

POLITICAL AND LEGAL RIGHTS

WE have already suggested (pp. 39, 42) that there is no ground to suspect unfairness in the elections for the Imperial Parliament at Westminster; and that the elections for the Parliament at Stormont, though somewhat biased in favour of better-off people by the retention of business property and university votes, are not to any effective degree 'gerrymandered' in favour of the Unionist Party. But more serious and persistent charges of gerrymandering are made about local government in several areas, and in particular about Londonderry. We therefore take this city as an example for detailed consideration, beginning with the case put forward by those who claim that deliberate discrimination is at work.

Londonderry is divided into three wards:

North, with two aldermen and six councillors, all Unionist
Waterside, with an alderman and three councillors, all Unionist
South, with two aldermen and six councillors, all Nationalist.

The South Ward is the largest, having on the 1961 register 10,749 electors, mostly Nationalist. There are 6,528 electors in North Ward, of whom about 66 per cent are Unionist; and 5,025 electors in Waterside Ward, of whom about 68 per cent are Unionist. Thus this ward division makes it possible to have a continuous Unionist majority on the Corporation, of 12 to 8, despite the fact that Unionists can claim the allegiance of only about 41 per cent of the population of voting age in the city, and Protestants constitute only about 37 per cent of the total population. It is further alleged that the shapes of the wards show that their boundaries were drawn so as to segregate an enormous Nationalist majority in the under-represented South Ward, and to make possible a Unionist majority in the other two; and that the policy of the Londonderry Corporation has been to prevent any building of houses by or lettings to Catholics in the Unionist wards, and to segregate all additions to the Catholic population as far as possible in the South Ward. Thus Alderman J. Hegarty, at the Corporation meeting on 28 July 1960, is reported to have said 'that protests had been made for many years about the segregation which had taken place in the allocation of houses in the city—Catholic tenants up to Creggan and Protestant tenants over to the Irish Street Estate or out to Northland'. Dealing with the Belmont Estate, Alderman Hegarty said: 'Up until recently only nine Catholics have succeeded in entering this Unionist stronghold which was built at public expense. Cases of terrible overcrowding and heart-breaking living conditions have been cynically pushed aside to bolster up this rotten little plot to keep this area Unionist.'[1]

There are several related allegations here, and they must be considered in turn.

(1) 'The composition of the Corporation does not reflect the wishes of the population of voting age.' This is true; the Unionist answer is that local authority ward boundaries must by law have regard to something more than the counting of heads, namely to the valuation of property in the area. This is asserted to be a requirement derived from the Towns Improvement (Ireland) Act, 1854, and adopted as a practice under the Local Government Act (N.I.), 1922; the latter Act followed British practice and abolished proportional representation, thus making it especially important to avoid anomalies in the electoral divisions. A large-scale alteration of electoral divisions therefore took place in 1923 all over the country, in the course of which a number of gross inequalities were removed.

The Londonderry divisions date, however, from 1936, in which year a proposal for a revision of the boundaries of the five wards then existing was made to the Ministry of Home Affairs. (There had been four wards from 1919 to 1922.) There was a public inquiry (at which the Nationalists were represented by Counsel), and an order was made which, in place of the proposal made to the Minister, divided the city into the present three wards. In accordance with the alleged requirements of the Act, which do not seem very clear, attention was paid both to numbers and to valuations, which at the time were as follows[2]:

---

[1] *Derry Journal*, 29 July 1960.
[2] See Senator A. J. Walmsley, *Northern Ireland: Its Policies and Record* (pamphlet published by the Ulster Unionist Council).

North Ward: Electors 5,469,   valuation £105,824
Waterside Ward: Electors 3,632,   valuation £35,079
South Ward: Electors 7,844,   valuation £63,065

It may be deduced that the formula used was roughly to equate an elector with £18 of valuation, and to provide one representative (including aldermen) for each 1,400 of the 'equivalent electors' so calculated. This would give the following numbers of representatives:

North	8·11
Waterside	3·99
South	8·11

—or 8, 4, and 8 to the nearest whole number. But there is, of course, no reason in law why this particular formula should have been used.

(2) 'The ward boundaries were drawn so as to concentrate Catholic voters in one ward.' This is an assertion about intentions, not capable of proof or disproof. The boundaries of Waterside Ward are geographically sensible, since this ward consists of the part of the city beyond the River Foyle. The other two wards are divided by a line which had already been defined for parliamentary elections. There is no doubt that it would be possible to find other divisions which would produce a different electoral result; this is a problem inherent in all systems of election by simple majority. But it must be remembered that the socially cohesive units or 'neighbourhoods' are in Northern Ireland liable to be mainly of one religion, so that any method of dividing up Londonderry which had regard to the social facts would tend to concentrate Catholic voters in some wards and Protestant voters in others. The arbitrariness of the results is greatly increased by having only three wards; if Unionist Waterside is regarded as a natural geographical area, the other two wards would be very likely to be one Protestant-Unionist and one Catholic-Nationalist.

(3) 'Since the boundaries were drawn, it has been the policy of the Corporation to keep Catholics out of the Unionist wards.' It is true in fact that this segregation has occurred; it would to some extent occur naturally, because of the distribution of churches and schools, but it is perhaps reasonable to expect that considerations

of electoral advantage will not have been wholly forgotten by the members of the Corporation. But, as we have shown (p. 114), the Londonderry Corporation and the Northern Ireland Housing Trust have together built within the city considerably more houses for Catholics than for Protestants. We have heard it suggested that the ratio is still inequitable, because of the much greater needs of the Catholic population; but it is significant that, despite the uncertainty which necessarily surrounds the continuance of Unionist rule in this historic outpost of the Plantation, so many houses should nevertheless have been built for Catholics.

It can be seen from this examination of the position in Londonderry that the alleged gerrymandering is either an accidental result or a deliberate exploitation of two decisions—to apply a British pattern of local government law to Northern Ireland, and to divide the city into only three wards. In order to throw more light on the situation, we have made inquiries from Unionists in the city, and find that 'alternative pleas' are made,

(a) that there is no gerrymandering, and

(b) that if there is, it is a good thing, for it is essential to keep the Nationalists out. Four reasons are offered for this view:

(i) that the attitude of Nationalists in Council meetings shows them to be unfit to have control of the Council. This reason perhaps underestimates the sobering effect of responsibility:

(ii) that Catholics have no right to speak of democracy, being subservient to an ecclesiastical dictatorship:

(iii) that franchise and representation should be based on responsibility, so that those who pay most rates should have the greatest say in how the money is spent. Catholic households and businesses probably contribute considerably less than half of the rates, perhaps little more than a third:

(iv) that Nationalist councillors are not honest in signing the declaration of allegiance required of members of the Corporation. Local government ought not to be in the hands of those who seek to engage in treason against Her Majesty.

The third of these reasons raises general questions about the 'rights of property', and there is room for difference of opinion about the right answers. The fourth reason involves important and deeply-held matters of political principle, and it is a cause for regret that so few non-Unionist commentators recognize the genuine strength of feeling in favour of the constitution. But it does not follow, of course, that treason can rightly be resisted by gerrymandering; a difficult conflict of principle is involved.

Charges of gerrymandering are also made about many other areas; thus Frank Gallagher, in *The Indivisible Island*, devotes a chapter (pp. 225–63) to the subject, mentioning (for instance) Strabane, Dungannon, Downpatrick, Clogher, Omagh, Enniskillen, Lisnaskea, and Armagh. The whole discussion, however, is based on the assumption that local government elections ought to be concerned solely with the counting of heads. Many people will agree with this assumption, but the fact remains that the law is thought to give certain ill-defined rights to property as well as to persons, and that in many areas Protestants own far more property than Catholics. It is open to Nationalists to argue that the Unionist attachment to the rights of property in local government affairs is simply a device to maintain their own control, but this is not an assertion capable of proof. It is our impression that the mixture of principle and self-interest which we have found in the London-derry situation will also be found in other areas where charges of 'gerrymandering' are made. On occasion, however, this charge is made as a form of abuse without any substantial evidence.

Portadown provides an example of a slightly different problem. The Borough Council (Urban Council before 1947) is elected by a single electoral area, returning twelve councillors and three alder-men. This would appear to favour block voting for the Unionist majority, and we have therefore investigated the origins of the system. Legally it is of course quite in order to have no division into wards; a similar system can exist in England under section 24 of the Local Government Act of 1933. The change in Portadown came into effect in 1936. A petition had been presented by the Urban Council to the Minister for Home Affairs to abolish the ward system, which (it was alleged) had been imposed by 'Dublin Castle' (i.e. by the Government of Ireland before partition) and was not fully democratic. It was better that every elector should have a chance of voting for every councillor. An objection was made at Council meetings by a much respected Catholic councillor, but this seems to have been related to procedural questions and not directly to the religious issue. Correspondence in the local press (e.g. *Portadown News*, 11 February 1933) referred to the change as though it were the undoing of a 'gerrymandering' under an Act of Lloyd George's Government.

Prior to the change there had been one Catholic councillor; he was re-elected in 1936, coming fifth on the list. No other Catholics stood. There was a period (1939–42) when under block voting two Catholics were returned; at the time of writing the non-Unionists consist of one member from the Ratepayers' Association and one from the Northern Ireland Labour Party, so that there is no direct representation of Catholics. But we think that on the evidence this has little to do with the lack of a division into wards: if the Catholic minority in Portadown desires to be represented on party lines, it would require proportional representation to ensure this.

We have referred to the large significance which is attached to a declaration of allegiance to the Queen. A similar feeling exists about the flying of the Union Jack, and about gatherings and processions intended to be a declaration of loyalty to Her Majesty. The right of assembly and the right to show flags and emblems therefore attract much political attention, and Nationalists (regarding them as general political rights) demand the privilege of showing their loyalty to another State by meetings, processions, and the flying of the flag of the Republic of Ireland. Other matters liable to generate heat are the right to play 'The Soldier's Song' and to remain seated when 'God Save the Queen' is played.

If these symbols of loyalty cause such high feelings that there is danger of a breach of the peace, it is appropriate that their use should be restricted, and the Northern Ireland Government has from time to time curbed the enthusiasm of members of both communities. Any such restriction is liable to be regarded as a monstrous infringement of basic political rights, and Unionists (in particular) consider it self-evident that a man should have the legal freedom to express his loyalty to the Queen anywhere within her dominions. Such attitudes provide a hard choice for those who have a duty to preserve the Queen's peace, and it is not easy to assess the validity of the judgements which they have reached.

Provision for the control of meetings and processions is now embodied in the Public Order (Northern Ireland) Act of 1951, while the right to prohibit the display of certain flags arises from the Flags and Emblems Act, 1954. There is, however, no right to prevent the display of the Union Jack, despite the fact that it is on occasion used as a party symbol rather than a declaration of unity. It is claimed by Nationalists that the law is used to suppress legitimate expressions of their feelings, while provocation by Orange processions is encouraged and protected. Thus we have been told that when a Nationalist band, parading in the Kilkeel area, was stoned by some Protestants, the police (instead of arresting those who threw the stones) arrested the band! (The facts of this incident, however, are complex and do not actually support this interpretation.) Mr. E. McAteer complained in the House of Commons on 22 March 1951 that a Nationalist procession had been diverted from its route in Londonderry, although Orange processions were freely permitted in a city which he claimed to be 60 per cent Nationalist. Mr. M. Morgan similarly complained on 3 May 1956 that police protection was given to an Orange band walking along the Longstone Road, Annalong, when the purpose of the march was to provoke the people of a predominantly Nationalist area. (There was a short period, in June 1952, when Orange bands were forbidden to use this route. Twelve of the Special Constables of the area resigned in protest.) Mr. J. F. Stewart objected (in the House of Commons, 9 May 1951) to the removal of 'the national flag' from the coffin of a member of the Irish Republican Brotherhood, at a funeral in Co. Tyrone. 'It is a flag', he said, 'for all Ireland, and . . . you people . . . should salute it, because the time is coming when you will do it anyway.' 'The Union Jack', said Senator J. G. Lennon on 23 March 1954, 'to us can never in Ireland be anything other than the hated symbol of thraldom and servitude.'

We have already referred (p. 63) to the incidents in Dungiven, where a procession by an Orange band was forbidden in 1959. We noted in the course of our inquiries that this had impressed Catholic opinion as being a fair-minded act, showing the willingness of the Unionists to keep their own 'lunatic fringe' in order. In 1960 the ban was lifted, and a serious skirmish was narrowly averted; this seems to have been due to an assembly of Nationalists from surrounding areas, rather than to the inhabitants of Dungiven itself.

It would in our view be unreasonable to expect a Unionist government to treat expressions both of loyalty and of disloyalty with that even-handed 'justice' which is demanded by Nationalist opinion. It is particularly difficult to expect them to restrict Orange processions, since these have a strong religious element. But it can be claimed that even an occasional willingness to restrict both sides is evidence of a desire to hold a fair balance between order and freedom, and that the absence of serious incidents shows that the object of restriction has been achieved. We think that the Nationalist objects are incidental to their general campaign against the constitution, rather than evidence of a harmful degree of discrimination.

Northern Ireland is sometimes referred to as a 'police state'. If this is meant to imply a parallel with foreign dictatorships, the implication is unfair. Dictators do not tolerate freedom of expression of views contrary to their own; but in Northern Ireland wide publicity is given to views which question the right of the State to any independent existence. In particular, there is a free and active Press. There are two Unionist morning papers in Belfast, the *Belfast News-Letter* and the *Northern Whig*, and a Nationalist morning paper, the *Irish News*; the *Irish Times*, representing Dublin upper-class opinion, also circulates in the North. The evening paper, the *Belfast Telegraph*, has a special position because (although it has Unionist connexions) it takes a liberal position and gives much publicity to non-Unionist views; it has a circulation of 200,000 all over the Province. Londonderry is served by three local papers, the *Standard*, the *Sentinel*, and the *Journal*; Enniskillen is the centre for that remarkable Unionist journal, the *Impartial Reporter*; and there are many other local and specialist weeklies. The British daily and Sunday newspapers, and the Dublin Sunday newspapers, also circulate in considerable numbers; the services of the B.B.C. and of Ulster Television give careful attention to the views of different parties; and those who wish can listen to Radio Eireann from across the Border. Ulster is certainly not insulated from new ideas by any form of censorship on means of communication.

Furthermore, the rule of law continues normally in almost all respects; the constitution contains important safeguards against discrimination on grounds of religion; and the law is interpreted by courts whose impartiality is generally accepted. The Supreme Court consists of a Court of Appeal and a High Court of Justice;

it has five judges of whom one is a Catholic. There are five County Court judges, of whom one is a Catholic. Professional residen magistrates deal with the minor cases. The Catholic community i strongly represented in the legal profession, and has an honoure place there.

The allegations of the existence of a 'police state' refer, in fact to the provisions for interrogation, search, and internment withou trial under the Special Powers Acts. The origins of these may b traced to events in the Irish Free State in 1922. In that yea members of the 'old' Sinn Fein party, led by de Valera, Catha Brugha, Austin Stack, and others, together with a large part o the 'old' Irish Republican Army, went into armed opposition t the Government led by Arthur Griffiths and Michael Collins because that Government was seeking to commit Ireland t acceptance of the Anglo-Irish Treaty. Thus began a period o 'troubles', which in Northern Ireland took the form of sporadi terrorism, attacks on 'British' rule, and counter-attacks o Nationalists. There were 232 people killed in the North, includin two Unionist members of Parliament, nearly 1,000 were injured and property to the value of some £3,000,000 was destroyed. As a means of dealing with these serious guerrilla attacks, whic used the advantage of a sympathetic or terrorized population, Civil Authorities (Special Powers) Act was passed in 1922. Thi gave the Minister for Home Affairs wide powers 'to take all suc steps and issue all such orders as may be necessary for preservin the peace' (section 1) and to proceed by making regulations. Th regulations subsequently made gave power to the police to stop interrogate, and search persons, and to stop vehicles, anywhere to search premises without a warrant; to seize certain property to close or render impassable roads, paths, ferries, or bridges without prior warning; to arrest people without warrant o suspicion of acting, having acted, or being about to act in manner contrary to the peace; and to hold such persons for a indefinite period without charge or trial.

In the words of Professor F. H. Newark,[4] this was 'a desperat

---

[3] From a booklet on the Civil Authorities (Special Powers) Act, issued by th Ministry of Home Affairs, 1948.

[4] In *Ulster under Home Rule*, ed. T. Wilson (Oxford University Press, 1955) p. 50.

measure taken to deal with a desperate situation'; and even stronger measures were imposed in the South, where the Government (in the words of Professor J. C. Beckett[5]) showed 'a ruthlessness which the British had never dared to display. They executed scores of prisoners and left hunger-strikers to starve if they chose'. Seventy-seven are said to have been executed in the South by shooting between November 1922 and May 1923, and two died in a prison hunger-strike. After the Easter rebellion in 1916, the British had executed sixteen men.

The Special Powers Act was renewed annually until 1933, and was then kept in force indefinitely by another Act, though the regulations under the Acts have been altered, repealed, or reinstated from time to time. The power of internment, however, was hardly used at all between the wars. The tradition of violent opposition lingered in the South, and the 'new' Irish Republican Army was at various times declared to be an unlawful organization. In 1924 the Irish Free State took power to imprison without trial, under a Public Safety Act; in the 1930's Coercion Acts allowed arrest and trial by military tribunals; in 1939 an Offences against the State Act was passed 'in comparison with which the Northern Ireland Statute almost pales in moderation'.[6]

Late in 1936 400 Thomson sub-machine guns were imported from the U.S.A., and the I.R.A. smuggled these and other weapons into Northern Ireland. In 1937 there was a province-wide recruiting campaign in the North for the I.R.A.; and in 1939 there was a series of bomb outrages in England, as a result of which seven people were killed and 137 injured. The Imperial Parliament in consequence passed a Prevention of Violence Act, which made it possible to arrest and detain suspected persons without a warrant. The signs of I.R.A. activity made it inevitable that measures should be taken to prevent hostile activity in Ulster during the war; the slogan 'England's extremity—Ireland's opportunity' on the walls of Belfast was a clear indication of the way in which some people were thinking and planning.

The numbers interned therefore rose considerably during the war years. But it is probable that terrorist activities grew in the

---

[5] *A Short History of Ireland* (Hutchinson, 1952), p. 183.

[6] J. Ll. J. Edwards, 'Special Powers in Northern Ireland', *Criminal Law Review*, 1956, p. 8.

1930's because of the disillusionment and suffering of long years o
unemployment, and at the end of the war Northern Ireland found
itself relatively prosperous. This may be why it proved possible
not only to release those interned, but to repeal a large number of
regulations under the Special Powers Acts. In 1949 no less than
forty-one were revoked; five new regulations were made in response to a brief outbreak of violence in 1950, but thirteen were
revoked in 1951, leaving only the bare framework of the Acts
ready to be rebuilt in case of emergency.[7]

In 1954 and 1955, however, new regulations were required to
deal with a series of armed raids; and in December 1956 troubles
of a more serious kind began to affect the Border areas. We reproduce below part of a manifesto issued by the 'Army Council of the
Irish Republican Army' on 12 December 1956:

'OGLAIG NA h-EIREANN
(Irish Republican Army)

TO THE IRISH PEOPLE.   *General Headquarters*

'Resistance to British rule in occupied Ireland has now entered a
decisive stage. Early today, Northern units of the Irish Republican Army
attacked key British occupation installations.

'Spearheaded by volunteers of the Irish Republican Army, our people
in the Six Counties have carried the fight to the enemy. They are the
direct victims of British Imperialism and they are also the backbone of
the national revolutionary resurgence.

'This is the age-old struggle of the Irish people versus British aggression. This is the same cause for which generations of our people have
suffered and died. In this grave hour, all Irish men and women, at home
and abroad, must sink their differences, political or religious, and rally
behind the banner of national liberation.

'We call on Irish men in the British Armed Forces to stand by the
motherland and refuse to bear arms against their own countrymen. We
call on members of the R.U.C. and B Special Constabulary to cease
being tools of British Imperialism and either stand on one side or join
us in the fight against tyranny. We warn them that should they reject
this plea they will be adjudged renegades by the Irish people and treated
accordingly by the Resistance Movement. . . .

'The whole of Ireland—its resources, wealth, culture, history and
tradition—is the common inheritance of all our people regardless of

[7] Newark, op. cit., p. 48.

religious belief. The division of this country by Britain, and its subjection to British political control in the north and to British economic domination in the south, must now be ended forever. It is up to this generation of Irish men and women to receive for all time our unity, independence, and freedom from foreign domination. The alternative, if the present situation continues, is extinction as a nation.

'The foe will use his considerable resources to divide us by fanning the fires of bigotry and sectarianism—twin enemies of Irish Republicanism. Let us be on our guard, a free Ireland cannot tolerate the one or the other. . . .

> ISSUED BY THE ARMY COUNCIL,
> IRISH REPUBLICAN ARMY.
> December 12th, 1956.'

It will be seen that this manifesto perpetuates the belief that it is the British 'occupying forces' which prevent Ulster from showing its true will to join with the Republic. In fact the small British forces have very little relation to the life of the Province; it is the strong will of a considerable majority of the people of Northern Ireland which sustains the present constitution. The I.R.A. was, however, careful to oppose religious bigotry, and to stand for the spirit of 1798, when Protestant Dissenters and Catholics stood side by side in rebellion. It was careful, too, not to provoke the civilian population; of 157 incidents involving fire-arms or explosives in the year following the manifesto, none was directed against the civil population.

In September 1958 the I.R.A. warned the Royal Ulster Constabulary and the Special Constabulary ('B Specials') that they were liable to attack, because they were aiding the British forces. Before this, however, attacks had been made on the police. An Ulster-based Republican group called *Saor Uladh* had been formed, allegedly by a former abstentionist member of the Northern Ireland Parliament, Liam Kelly, who was later a member of the Senate of the Republic of Ireland. Saor Uladh is believed to have been responsible for a number of minor bomb attacks against customs posts, Post Office vans, and police barracks (i.e. stations), commencing in 1955. Some of its members were killed in 1958 in attacks on the Rosslea police barracks and in a gun battle on the railway line near Newtownbutler. Kelly is understood to have spent periods in the Republic, and to have been held for questioning by the Garda Siochana on several occasions; but no charge could be brought against him, since Saor Uladh is not illegal in the Republic. We are told that the I.R.A. regarded Saor Uladh as a collection of dangerous amateurs who rushed into ill-planned operations; irritation between the two bodies may have been increased by Saor Uladh tapping some traditional sources of I.R.A. money in the United States. (The irresponsible generosity of Irish Americans, supporting in their mother country terrorist activities which they would probably condemn if they saw them at close quarters, has long been a harmful influence on Irish affairs.)

Other 'splinter groups' with violent aims appeared from time to time; for instance the blowing up of the lock gates of the Newry ship canal in 1958, which caused serious unemployment among Catholic workers in Newry, was attributed to a group called the 'McCrystal Boys', who were impatient with the restraint shown by the I.R.A. The physical effect of the various campaigns was to cause repeated damage, mostly of a minor kind, to bridges, customs posts, police barracks, etc., and to cause a small loss of life (nineteen dead from 1956 to the end of 1961). The psychological effect, in creating suspicion and hatred, especially in the Border areas, was much greater. Both sides feel strongly about their dead. Thus Senator A. J. Walmsley, speaking in Dublin on 27 February 1959, said:

'Since 1921 you have made constant attacks on us with bomb, bullet and pen. You have murdered many of our people. Your marauders have widowed many young mothers and left many of our children orphaned, and those who lost their lives at the hands of our defence forces returned to a civic funeral and a heroes' grave. You have not recognised your obligations under international law. You have flouted the conventions of civilised people by allowing those who have murdered, robbed, maimed and destroyed in my country to walk your streets without let or hindrance.'[8]

The opposite view is shown by the comments of *The Kerryman* on an attack by the 'North Fermanagh Resistance column' on Brookeborough police barracks on New Year's Day, 1957, when Sean Sabhat and Feargal O'Hanlon died.

[8] Walmsley, op. cit., p. 4.

'Sabhat and O'Hanlon, young men of exemplary lives, imbued with the very highest of patriotic motives, have gone down to early graves because they believed that physical force, as the last resort, was the only means by which the unity of the country could be effected. . . . Their deeds and their memories will be honoured by a virile, uncompromising section of our people. Rightly or wrongly, they are determined that this question of partition will not be relegated or ignored.'[9]

But another and more representative view from the South is given by the statement of the Taoiseach (Prime Minister), Mr. Lemass, when I.R.A. members killed Constable Norman Anderson with seventeen bullets at Annaghmartin, as he was returning from a visit to his fiancée:

'The news of the brutal murder of this young Irishman will be received by all Irish people with horror and disgust. The attitude of the Government to crimes of this character has been clearly and frequently stated. I urge all Irishmen who value the good name of our country to do everything within their power to prevent any possibility of the repetition of this foul deed and to bring its perpetrators to justice.'[10]

Despite the continuance of occasional incidents, in 1961 the Northern Ireland Government once again felt in a strong enough situation to release suspected I.R.A. members and sympathizers from internment. The numbers detained at various periods were as follows:[11]

			1930	Nil	1940	302	1950	7	1960	144
			1	Nil	1	73	1	13	1	Nil
			2	Nil	2	243	2	Nil		
			3	Nil	3	112	3	Nil		
			4	Nil	4	12	4	Nil		
			5	2	5	3	5	Nil		
1926	Nil		6	Nil	6	Nil	6	Nil		
7	Nil		7	Nil	7	Nil	7	123		
8	Nil		8	Nil	8	Nil	8	187		
9	Nil		9	Nil	9	82	9	Nil	9	159

[9] Quoted in J. McGarrity, *Resistance: the Story of the Struggle in British-Occupied Ireland* (Irish Freedom Press, 1957).

[10] Reported in the *Irish Times*, 28 January 1961.

[11] W. A. Carson, *Ulster and the Irish Republic* (W. W. Cleland (Belfast), 1956), p. 24, statements in House of Commons, 7 May 1958 and 25 January 1961, *Belfast Telegraph*, 8 March 1960, and private information. It is not clear to which date in the year some of the figures relate, and they should therefore be taken as giving only a rough indication of changes.

For a period (1957–9) I.R.A. suspects were interned by the Government of the Republic at the Curragh, and there has at all times been some co-operation between the Royal Ulster Constabulary and the Garda Siochana in tracing suspects. On the other hand, there is no recognized way of extraditing offenders from the Republic to Northern Ireland—the Extradition Act of 1870 does not apply between these two areas, and in any case the Act does not cover political offences. It is felt by many in Northern Ireland that 'members of illegal organizations' who are arrested in the Republic receive sentences of derisory shortness.

The problem raised by the Special Powers Acts is a conflict between political theory and practical necessity. A Commission appointed by the (British) National Council for Civil Liberties concluded, in 1936, that:

'. . . the existing conditions of rule—secured by the supersession of representative government and the abrogation of the rule of law and the liberty of the subject, the bases of Special Powers—cannot be described otherwise than as totally un-British. It is clear to the Commission that the way to the re-establishment of constitutional government, the prerequisite of law and order in democratic communities, can be paved only by the repeal of the Special Powers Acts. Wherever the pillars of constitutional rule, Parliamentary sovereignty and the rule of law are overthrown there exist the essential conditions of dictatorship. It is sad that in the guise of temporary and emergency legislation there should have been created under the shadow of the British Constitution a permanent machine of dictatorship—a standing temptation to whatever intolerant or bigoted section may attain power to abuse its authority at the expense of the people it rules.'[12]

These strong words seem wholly unrealistic to those who have the responsibility of maintaining law and order. Their attitude is that no effective alternative to the use of the Special Powers Acts

---

[12] *Report of a Commission of Inquiry appointed to examine the purpose and effect of the Civil Authorities (Special Powers) Acts (Northern Ireland) 1922 and 193.* (National Council for Civil Liberties, 1936), p. 40. Of this report Professor Newark (op. cit., p. 49) remarks '. . . this was a remarkable production. In the blue paper cover with all the format of a Government Blue Book it was calculated to deceive the unwary into believing that in some way it emanated from Whitehall'. St. John Ervine (*Craigavon*, p. 534) says: 'The Report issued by this collection of disgruntled cranks is a scandalous document.'

has ever been proposed; that the Acts have on more than one occasion succeeded in suppressing terrorism; and that in recent years Northern Ireland has been remarkably fortunate in avoiding a chain reaction of reprisals, which would have been almost certain to occur if measures of control had not been used. It is admitted that the Special Powers are for emergency use only, that the regulations should be repealed as soon as it is safe to do so, and that internment without trial should end as quickly as possible. An internee could in recent years obtain his freedom at any time on signing one or other of the following official declarations:

'I . . . solemnly declare that although I was a member of . . . from . . . to . . . . I have now severed all connexion with it and I do not intend to have anything further to do with that organization or any other illegal organization, or assist them in any way in the future.'

'I . . . hereby declare that I have never been, am not now, and never intend to become a member of the I.R.A. or any other illegal organization, or to assist any such organization in the future, and I am prepared to go before a court, if necessary, and swear that this is the truth.'

Those who on grounds of principle have refused to make either of these declarations have on occasion been released without conditions; it is by this means that the internees were finally cleared in 1961. There has also been a provision by which an internee could make a case for his release before a tribunal, with a lawyer in the chair.

Dr. Edwards[13] sums up the difficulty by pointing out that the regulations are in several respects repugnant to traditional conceptions of the law and its enforcement, but that 'what is wanted is that those who do not live in the midst of these exceptional conditions should properly appreciate the case for the retention of the special powers'. The best way to stop the use of the special powers was adopted by the I.R.A. in 1962, when it abandoned its campaign.

The purpose of the Special Powers is to prevent incidents which would cause hatred and strife between different parts of the community; yet the application of the powers is itself inflammatory, so that a choice has to be made between two evils. Those whose husbands and sons have been held in prison for years without trial can hardly be expected to look kindly on the Northern Ireland

[13] Op. cit., pp. 11, 16.

constitution. Interrogations frequently take place during the nigh
or early morning, when the person required is likely to be at home
and when arrests can be made without disturbance. We have hear
a number of complaints of onerous and unnecessary interrogations
but we have no evidence that what is done goes beyond the neces
sities of effective police action. There are also complaints of damag
done during police searches (which frequently reveal dumps c
arms); and it is alleged that no compensation is given for such
damage, even to innocent parties. The nuisance of interrogatio:
and search is of course carried mainly by the Catholic community
since it is there that contacts with the I.R.A. are likely to be found

We have also heard recent complaints of wrongful or unneces
sary internment, similar to those mentioned in the Civil Libertie
report of 1936. On these again we have no strong evidence; we do
not know if it is alleged that the men detained were not allowed t
make the official declaration, or if they refused to do so—the latte
would of course suggest that the internment was in accordanc
with normal policy. Some complaints of interference with lega
activities have been made—for instance, the watching of meetings
and questioning about wholly legal organizations. The cases know:
to us are, however, such that it would not be unreasonable to expec
infiltration by the I.R.A.: and it may well be that the police actio:
was reasonable.

More serious are the allegations of police brutality. Four me:
arrested for questioning after the murder of Sergeant Ovens by
booby-trap in a disused house alleged that they were repeatedl
beaten, starved, questioned for long periods, and finally forced t
sign a false admission; five youths arrested in Armagh in 195
stated that they were put in tubs of cold water for more than tw
hours, and beaten with rubber truncheons while standing nake
before their interrogators.[14] In the Ovens case two men were trie
for murder, but (there being apparently some doubt about th
validity of the confessions) they were acquitted; they were imme
diately interned, but have since been released. We do not kno
where the truth lies on these matters. It seems to us likely that o:
occasion the police will use rough treatment against those who are
after all, trying to kill them; and that in the Ovens case it was
mistake to conduct the interrogation at the barracks at which Oven

[14] Quoted in McGarrity, op. cit., pp. 92–4.

as stationed. On the other hand, we have been advised by people who have gone through periods of questioning and imprisonment that it is easy to exaggerate and misinterpret the facts.

Evil breeds evil; the attempt to change the will of a proud people by terrorism is bound to lead to an abridgement of political rights. But, to set matters in perspective, it must be remembered that most of the population of Northern Ireland have in recent years gone about their ordinary business unaffected by the attacks and little aware of the restrictions. To the Unionist, this proves the value of the Special Powers Acts; to some of their opponents, that they are not needed.

CHAPTER 9

THE TRADE UNION MOVEMENT AND SECTARIANISM

THERE are rather over 200,000 trade union members in Northern Ireland.[1] As elsewhere, the basic unit of trade union organization is the branch, which is formed of members in a particular district, or at a particular place of work, or (occasionally) in a particular section of the trade. Most of the branches belong to unions with headquarters in England (or Scotland), but some have headquarters in Northern Ireland, and a few are based in the Republic. Mr. David Bleakley, in a paper read in Belfast to the Statistical and Social Inquiry Society of Ireland in 1954 (but unfortunately unpublished), distinguished sixty-eight British-based unions, covering 90 per cent of the membership, nineteen Northern Ireland unions, and five Republic-based unions. Forty per cent of all unionists were in the Amalgamated Transport and General Workers' Union (part of the T. and G.W.U., with headquarters in London); next came the Amalgamated Engineering Union and the National Union of General and Municipal Workers. Two Northern Ireland-based unions, the Transport and Allied Operatives' Union and the Civil Service Association, had more than 5,000 members. The Republic-based unions were small, with about 9,000 members between them.

Some twenty-eight British unions also have members in the Republic, and an important section of the trade union movement has always regarded workers' solidarity within Ireland as an ideal not to be frustrated by a political border. In 1894 an Irish Trade Union Congress was formed, composed both of Irish unions and of Irish branches of British unions. This continued to serve the whole of Ireland after partition, about 60 per cent of its members in recent times[2] having been in the North. All the important

---

[1] The statistics vary according to the definitions used, particularly about the unions of 'white collar' workers.

[2] I.e. after the foundation of the Congress of Irish Unions; see below.

British-based unions, with the exception of the United Pattern-makers' Association and the Amalgamated Society of Woodcutting Machinists, were affiliated to the Irish Congress, and so were all the Republic-based unions operating in the North with the exception of the Irish Bank Officials' Association. The four largest Northern Ireland-based unions, on the other hand, were not affiliated. In 1945 twenty-two unions which were active only in Ireland formed a Congress of Irish Unions; by 1958 the I.T.U.C. had 226,000 members in sixty-six unions and the C.I.U. 188,000 in twenty-one unions.[3] In 1959, however, after prolonged negotiations, the two trade union bodies reunited in the Irish Congress of Trade Unions, membership of which is open to unions with headquarters in any part of Ireland, and to unions based outside Ireland provided they give certain rights of autonomy to their Irish members. Within the I.C.T.U. there is provision for a separate Northern Ireland conference and a Northern Ireland Committee, all of whose members in fact belong to unions with headquarters in Britain.

Union organization in Northern Ireland thus reproduces all the complexities found in Britain, such as the existence of general, industrial, and craft unions of very various sizes, and it adds a number of complexities of its own. The situation is further complicated because there is no single political movement which is predominant among the Irish workers. The great figures in Irish working-class movements are James Connolly, executed after the Easter rising in 1916, and Jim Larkin. There can be no doubt of their views on partition: for instance, Connolly wrote:

'Belfast is bad enough as it is; what it would be under (Orange) rule the wildest imagination cannot conceive.'

'The effect of such exclusion (i.e. partition) upon labour in Ireland will be . . . disastrous. All hopes of uniting the workers, irrespective of religion or old political battle cries, will be shattered, and through North and South the issue of Home Rule will still be used to cover the iniquities of the capitalist and landlord class. I am not speaking without due knowledge of the sentiments of the organized Labour movement in Ireland when I say that we would much rather see the Home Rule Bill defeated than see it carried with Ulster or any part of Ulster left out.'[4]

[3] Ruaidhri Roberts, 'Trade Union Organisation in Ireland', *Journal of the Statistical and Social Inquiry Society of Ireland*, 1958–9, p. 95.

[4] *Forward*, 21 March and 11 April 1914: quoted in *Socialism and Nationalism* (Dublin, Three Candles Press, 1948), pp. 109, 114–15.

The appeal of socialism in the Connolly tradition to Irish labour has, however, been offset by two other strong influences. One is the teaching of the Catholic Church, generally sympathetic to the just claims of the working class but not to ideas of revolution or anything of the nature of Communism. The other is the importance of the constitutional issue in the North, which produces an allegiance either to the Unionist Party or to one of the Nationalist organizations. As we have seen (p. 50), the Northern Ireland Labour Party occupies a difficult position between the opposing extremes, and it cannot rely on the weight of trade union support which sustains the British Labour Party. Communist influence is very small, though there are some influential individual Communists in the unions.

The trade union movement's many connexions with the South make it politically suspect to official Unionism. The Minister of Labour refused to recognize either the Irish Congress of Trade Unions or its Northern Committee, because of their connexions with another State, and there has therefore been no regular channel by which the unions can make known a united view to the Government. For thirteen years (1946–59) the Northern Ireland Government refused to follow the lead of Westminster in repealing the Trades Disputes Act of 1927, and this tardiness was particularly resented by the unions, and was regarded as a form of discrimination against them. The difficulty about relations with government is not that the trade unions are anti-Unionist, but that they contain all shades of opinion—Communist and Catholic, Nationalist and Unionist—and do not fit into the neat divisions usually drawn across Ulster life.

In fact, the unions have in general taken a stand against religious sectarianism, and have provided a place of meeting and common action for Protestant and Catholic. Trade union members as individuals may be strong in their religious loyalties and perhaps even unreasonable in their beliefs, fears, and hatreds; but in the corporate work of the union the solidarity of the members takes first place, and those who are active in union affairs often find, very naturally, that they grow to understand and appreciate their fellow-members of opposite religion.

This does not mean, however, that the unions are wholly unmarked by religious differences. We have already referred (p. 103) to the division in the Port of Belfast, where cross-Channel boats are unloaded by members of the Amalgamated Transport and General Workers' Union, who happen to be mainly Protestant, while the deep-sea traffic (incidentally, not such regular work) is handled by members of the Irish Transport and General Workers' Union, almost all Catholic. In general, the religious affiliation of union members can be regarded as related to the kind of work they do— relatively more unskilled workers are Catholics, and therefore a union with many unskilled members tends to have a higher proportion of Catholics. We have obtained some evidence which illustrates this point by finding the religious affiliations of the 379 branch secretaries (in 1959) of fifty-three of the unions operating in the Province; the only large unions not covered were the Ulster Transport and Allied Operatives' Union and the Northern Ireland Civil Service Association, with about 8,000 and 5–6,000 members respectively, so the results may be regarded as a fair representation of the division, by religion, of a sample of the most active members of the trade union movement.

Twenty per cent of the branch secretaries were Catholic and 80 per cent Protestant. The Catholic proportion was, however, 46 per cent in the large Amalgamated Transport and General Workers' Union, with its considerable unskilled membership; it was only 12 per cent in the Amalgamated Engineering Union and 9 per cent in the Association of Supervisory Staffs, Executives, and Technicians, while there were no Catholic branch secretaries of the Boilermakers' union. The building unions tended to show a somewhat higher Catholic proportion, while the attraction of jobs under the Westminster Government is reflected in the Catholic proportion for the Union of Post Office Workers (57 per cent). The National Union of General and Municipal Workers, however, is believed to have about 90 per cent Protestants among its branch secretaries, despite its unskilled membership; and we are told that this may reflect the discrimination by local authorities in Northern Ireland. The split in education is reflected in the difference between the Ulster Teachers' Union (mainly Protestant) and the Irish National Teachers' Organization (mainly Catholic, with headquarters in the Republic). Geographical effects are shown by the fact that, of fifteen branch secretaries in the Newry area, thirteen are Catholic.

There are also influences (in addition to the political parties) tending to divide workers on sectarian lines. Thus there are 'Loyal Workers' Associations' in the aircraft and shipbuilding industries, and a 'Catholic Protection Society' in the aircraft factory.* A new divisive influence is Ulster Protestant Action (see page 48), one of whose objects is to keep Protestant and loyal workers in employment in times of depression, in preference to their Catholic fellow-workers. This movement is capable of rapid expansion at a time of economic difficulty,[5] and it caused the unions some disquiet when it held anti-Catholic demonstrations at the shipyard gates just before the Twelfth of July holidays in 1959. The Northern Ireland Committee of the Irish Congress of Trade Unions issued a press statement calling on trade unionists not to associate with such activity, and sought meetings with Church leaders to discuss corporate action which might discourage sectarian feeling. At the Northern Ireland Conference of the Congress in May 1960 the following resolution was passed:

'This Conference declares its opposition to all forms of discrimination on the basis of race, religion, sex, colour or politics, as such discrimination or segregation leads to strife and often loss of life. The Conference calls upon all Trade Unionists to oppose discrimination wherever it may raise its head and to practise tolerance, equality and justice.'

It seems reasonable, therefore, to regard the signs of religious difference within the trade union movement as secondary, the natural result of the other divisions in the Province, and to consider the movement as being an important uniting influence.

[5] Up to mid-1962, however, it has shown no signs of such a development.

* [Add. 1972] After publication in 1962 we received a denial of the existence of a 'Catholic Protection Society' in the aircraft factory, and on further inquiry we found that the reference had been to a branch factory during the 1939–45 war. In fact, communal relations in the shipyards and the aircraft factory have remained remarkably good throughout recent troubles.

CHAPTER 10

RELIGIOUS DIFFERENCES
AND LEISURE-TIME ACTIVITIES

THE things which people do with their leisure—whether they are cultural, social, or athletic activities, or the pursuit of amusement—are often done in company with their neighbours and friends. Therefore the division in Northern Ireland society has a natural derived effect on leisure-time activities. We generally expect to find Protestants playing games with Protestants, and Catholics meeting their fellow church-members in social clubs. What is interesting is to look for the influences which are not simply a natural derivative from the social situation. Some of these have the effect of uniting people in a common interest which transcends the religious division; others make the division more definite, through institutions and habits of thought which are directly related to the use of leisure.

Before considering particular examples, it is worth while to make some general points about the attitudes of the churches to the use of leisure:

1. Christianity means a lot to the people of Northern Ireland, and one aspect of religion which is often and rightly stressed is that Christian discipleship is a matter of the whole of life, and not just of church attendance on Sundays. One way of giving expression to this truth is to seek social life and recreations within a particular church congregation—and in consequence to limit one's contacts with people of other denominations. There is a vigorous growth of church clubs, fellowships, and societies covering a bewildering variety of activities, and it is certainly possible for many people to find all the corporate activities they need for their leisure time without going outside their own church.

2. The Protestant community shows strong signs of the influence which is commonly called 'puritanical'. A 'good-living' man, in the Ulster phrase, is decent and sober; in former times he would have resisted the temptations of the theatre, the cinema, and the

dance-hall. Outdoor sports have long been liberated from this sus-picion of evil, but there are still a few who have doubts about listening to secular music. Such attitudes go with a strong tem-perance movement, and with total opposition to betting and gam-bling. There is, of course, a strong Catholic temperance move-ment; but on the other hand there are many moderate drinkers among Catholic priests as well as lay people, and gambling has for long been used as a means of raising money for Catholic causes. Gambling is socially more acceptable among Catholics than among Protestants; and a large proportion of owners of 'bars' (i.e. public houses) and betting shops is drawn from the Catholic community.

3. A Catholic is prepared to use Sunday for recreation, provided he has first attended Mass; in general he will see nothing wrong in paying for entry to organized Sunday games and amusements. Few Protestants will in the sight of their neighbours engage in Sunday recreation, even in so harmless a form as digging the garden. This different attitude to Sunday means that many Protestants never see or join in the Gaelic games and the dances which are a common feature of Catholic Sunday amusements.

4. We have remarked (pp. 85–86) that Catholics, with some justification, regard the secular State schools as Protestant schools. The tendency to classify all that is not specifically Catholic as Protestant (and therefore dangerous) is, however, a general one in some Catholic circles. An activity which seems to a Protestant quite non-denominational and unrelated to religion—say, a wood-working class—may come under the suspicion of a zealous priest as involving a dangerous degree of mixing, and Catholic members will be asked to stay away. Our attention has been drawn to a number of leading men and women in Ulster public life who have been criticized by their fellow-Catholics, and regarded as dangerously advanced in their views, because they have shared in secular activities with Protestants.

But, despite all these divisive influences, a strong special interest still has power to unite people; and this is particularly true in the practice and appreciation of the arts, in which group labels are readily forgotten. We find no consciousness of religious differences in the Royal Ulster Academy of Arts or in the Ulster Society of Women Artists; in the Belfast Philharmonic Society or the Grand

Opera Society of Northern Ireland; in the Poetry Society or the P.E.N. Centre. (The latter has at the moment only one known Catholic member out of about forty, but there have been others in the recent past.) The Group Theatre, the Little Theatre, the Lyric Theatre, and the Arts Theatre in Belfast have had Catholics among their notable players, and yet have retained the support of theatre-going Protestants. The Lyric Theatre drama school (for children) is mixed. Folk dancing also gets support from both communities.

In amateur drama, however, we find that separate groups often exist for Protestants and Catholics. We have traced two Protestant groups and a Catholic group in Portadown: one of each in Newry and Downpatrick: two light operatic and drama societies in Londonderry: and a Catholic drama group in Ardglass, the Protestant group having disbanded. These separate societies, however, may be willing to co-operate for a drama festival or a Feis.

The Council for the Encouragement of Music and the Arts, a Government-subsidized body which is roughly the Northern Ireland equivalent of the Arts Council, has run into political difficulty in Londonderry and Newry, mostly over the requirement that the national anthem should be played at concerts which it sponsors. But in other places (for instance, Newcastle, County Down) it has obtained the co-operation of both communities, and a number of chairmen of its local committees are Catholics.

As far as we can discover, most social clubs for adults are not mixed. Many are, of course, connected with churches; those that are not often get their nucleus from members of one community, and someone from the other group then feels insecure, lonely, and unwanted if he attends. But the passion for bridge transcends sectarian difficulties—in both Newry and Portadown, for instance, the Bridge Clubs are mixed. Organizations which belong to an international movement are often mixed, perhaps because the principles for selecting the membership are not locally decided. Thus some Rotary Clubs are mixed—and, of course, the Rotary movement is also active in the Republic, and counts as a distinguished member the Taoiseach (Prime Minister), Mr. Lemass. But in places Catholics have been told that 'the Church will provide you with all the fellowship and friendship and service you require'; as a result the Rotary movement has been unable to develop in some centres. We find also that (for some reason) the Belfast Rotary Club is wholly or largely Protestant in its membership. There is mixing in the groups of the Round Table, in many Young Farmers' Clubs, in the Youth Hostels Association, in the British Legion, in the Business and Professional Women's Clubs, and among the Soroptimists.

Mixing of the sexes in youth clubs is less common in Northern Ireland than in Great Britain; where it occurs, there would be great obstacles to obtaining members from both communities, because of the fear of mixed marriages. The large and active 'Newsboys' Club' in Belfast was started in the nineteen-twenties by Toc H as a club for the boys who sold the evening papers, and it was from the beginning mixed in religion. It broke up during the riots of 1935, and was restarted on the basis that if a group of Protestants wanted to join they must bring along an equal number of Catholics. 'Old boys' of the club of both faiths serve on the guiding committee. Clubs of this kind are, however, in a minority, because much of the youth work of the Province is based on individual church congregations. Thus, of 42 clubs affiliated to the National Association of Boys' Clubs, 21 are Protestant, 14 Catholic, and 7 fully mixed in religion. We gather that in addition some 'Protestant' clubs have a few Catholic members, and vice versa. However, clubs whose members are of opposite persuasions do on occasion meet in games, attend each other's entertainments, and share in common training courses for youth leaders. The informal activities of youth in the commercial dance-halls are of course free from any distinctions on grounds of religion, but we have not been able to assess which community uses these dance-halls most.

The television and radio are, in Ulster as elsewhere, an important leisure-time influence; and the success of the B.B.C. and Ulster Television in keeping a balance in their programmes may perhaps be judged by the fact that they are criticized by both sides. The Catholic objection is primarily concerned with employment and politics. It is said that no Catholics are employed in senior positions in the B.B.C. in Belfast. Ulster Television has some Catholic influence on its Board; the top management is Protestant, but there are Catholics in prominent positions on both technical and programme presentation sides. It is also said that Nationalist political views do not get a fair hearing. As far as election times are concerned, this complaint is made by all small political parties, and there seems little reason to suppose that the Nationalists are subjected to any special discrimination. At other times, minority views are given quite a substantial place in various discussion programmes.

The Protestant complaints are religious, and are probably based on a fear of the effectiveness of the appeal of Catholic ritual when presented on television, and on the frequent references to Catholicism in televised American films. In 1959 the Western Presbytery of the Reformed Presbyterian Church (a small Calvinist group) protested to the B.B.C. about 'the increased facilities which are being afforded both on radio and on television for Romanist propaganda'. In the same year the Dean of Dromore was reported as referring to 'disturbing Roman Catholic propaganda' on radio and television; he said that 'where religion was discussed Roman Catholics put on their best controversialists'. In fact there is no ground for complaint about there being too many Catholic services broadcast or televised, and the B.B.C. can hardly be expected to reduce the number because the services make an effective appeal. The division of time is illustrated by the following figures of sound radio services broadcast on Sundays by the B.B.C. in Northern Ireland in 1961:

	Actual Number	Number if Services had been distributed in proportion to Sizes of Denominations
Church of Ireland	17	13
Presbyterian	20	16
Roman Catholic	9	19
Methodist	5	3
Baptist	1	⎫
Reformed Presbyterian	1	⎬ 3 (all others)
Plymouth Brethren	1	⎭
	54	54

Interest in sport is strong in Northern Ireland. In terms of numbers, of course, most of the interest is that of spectators rather than participants, and at the bigger sporting events people can forget about religion in the anonymity of the crowd. Rugby football, hockey, cricket, tennis, bowls, and golf are organized on an all-Ireland basis, with Northern and Southern branches affiliated to a single Board of Control, and playing in international competitions as a single side. In the Republic all these games are played both by Catholics and by Protestants, and (in particular) many leading Catholic schools (especially in the Dublin area) play Rugby football, hockey, tennis, and cricket. It might be thought, therefore, that sport would be a unifying influence, but this is only part of the truth.

The Catholic schools in the North do not (in general) play Rugby football or cricket, which are referred to by those of Nationalist opinion as 'foreign', 'Protestant', or 'British' games. There are several reasons for this. The playing of team games at school was originally a preserve of the rich, and was therefore associated with the Protestant Ascendancy. Much of the pioneering work in Catholic secondary education in Ulster has been done by the Christian Brothers, and this order supports Gaelic games (though it allows Association football). The Jesuits, who might have taken a different view, have no schools in the Province. The support for Gaelic games is also part of a movement of protest with strong historical origins, which we must now describe.

A Gaelic game with a long authentic tradition is hurling or hurley, a kind of hockey played with a large flat-headed stick. The same tradition is claimed for Gaelic football, played with a Soccer ball, and occupying a position somewhere between Rugby and Association football—the ball can be handled but not carried beyond three steps. Such sports naturally aroused enthusiasm among those who desired to see Ireland an independent nation, and in 1884 the Gaelic Athletic Association was founded to preserve and promote Gaelic sports. One of the founders, Michael Cusack, wrote in the *United Irishman* at the time an appeal to Irish people 'to take the management of their games in their own hands, to encourage and promote in every way every form of athletics which is particularly Irish, and to remove in one sweep everything foreign and iniquitous in the present system'; he wished to see British influences on sport removed, 'the corrupting influences which for several years have been devastating the sporting grounds of our cities and towns and are fast spreading to our rural population'.[1]

Many of the Catholic clergy were strong supporters of the new

---

[1] Quoted in James Hurley, 'The Founders of the Gaelic Athletic Association', *Capuchin Annual*, 1960, p. 196, from *United Irishman*, 11 October 1884.

movement, but (to the embarrassment of some of them) so were the political extremists, and it is said that many a gathering of a County Board of the League, when the clergy had left, would resolve itself into a business meeting of the Irish Republican Brotherhood. British soldiers and police were expressly excluded from the League, and, in order to maintain a united national spirit, a ban was imposed on League members playing, watching, or helping certain non-Gaelic games. This ban, which was against the wishes of the League's first patron, Archbishop Croke, is still of importance, and is partially enforced through Vigilance Committees whose membership is secret.[2] The Catholic schools originally played Gaelic games as evidence of a patriotic and nationalist spirit, and their patriotism would have been in doubt if they had not held to the intention of the G.A.A.'s ban; but nowadays the continuation of Gaelic games in schools is mainly a matter of tradition.

As far as we can find out, the present state of support in Northern Ireland for the principal games is as follows:

1. *Rugby football* is played mainly by Protestants, but occasional Catholics who have played the game at schools in the South join Ulster sides. The 'Ireland' team has members of both religions and represents both North and South; international games arouse great interest among all parts of the community.

2. *Association football* is played by members of both communities, and Catholic schools on occasion play against other schools. The game has a large following in Belfast, and there used to be some sectarian trouble over games between Linfield, a Protestant club, and Celtic, a Belfast club with strong Catholic support. (Similar trouble is of course a feature of certain games in Glasgow.) The Celtic club was, however, disbanded in 1951, following an incident at a game and a change of policy by the management. There is now no club which is a figure-head for the Catholic community, and on the whole Protestants and Catholics co-operate, both as players and as club supporters.

There is a long-standing dispute about international Association football matches. For the purpose of matches with England, Scotland, or Wales the Irish Football Association can pick players from both sides of the Border (including, for instance, men born in the Republic playing for English or Scottish sides). In practice pressure

---

[2] *Irish Times*, 28 November 1961, and *The Freeman*, 2 November 1885.

has been brought on players from the South to refuse to play for the 'Ireland' side, and the team is now picked from the North only. The body which deals with matches outside the British Isles (the F.I.F.A.) recognizes the Republic of Ireland and Northern Ireland as two separate countries.

3. *Gaelic football* is said to be played by over 2,800 clubs and by 200,000 players in all Ireland, excluding school and college sides; and it draws crowds of over 80,000 to Croke Park in Dublin. It is almost exclusively a game for Catholics, and in Belfast Protestants are usually unaware of what goes on or of the names of the clubs. The games at Roger Casement Park would naturally be avoided by Protestants, both because they take place 'up the Falls Road' in a Catholic area, and because the main events are on Sunday. In the provinces there is more Protestant interest in the success of a local club, but we gather that few Protestants actually go to see a game. (The Down team won the all-Ireland championship in both 1960 and 1961, and this roused much enthusiasm in the county.) Gaelic football, incidentally, continues in the summer.

4. *Hockey* is played mainly by Protestants, but it finds a place in Catholic girls' schools and in consequence some Catholics play in the senior women's sides. The international team represents both North and South; Northern players have also been chosen for British Olympic sides. Hurling and the corresponding Gaelic women's game, Camogie, are normally played by Catholics only.

5. *Cricket* is also organized on an all-Ireland basis, and Catholics from Southern schools are to be found in the Gentlemen of Ireland side. The game has a middle-class following, but it also has strong general support in some localities—for instance, Waringstown, Lurgan, Donacloney, and Comber. In the villages around Londonderry (for instance, Ardmore, Donemena and Sion Mills) the game arouses the keen interest of both communities and both Protestants and Catholics are to be found in the teams.

6. *Tennis* is organized on an all-Ireland basis, and Northern Ireland players therefore qualify for inclusion in the Irish Davis Cup side. Many clubs are however attached to churches, and there is not therefore much mixing of members of different faiths within clubs, though clubs of the two communities play one another in organized competitions.

7. *Bowling* owes its popularity to the strong Scottish influence

in the North, and 90 per cent of the bowlers in Ireland belong to the three Bowling Associations in Ulster. These associations are affiliated to an all-Ireland body, and there are a number of clubs which show cordial relations between members of different faiths. Nevertheless this game is mainly played by Protestants.

8. *Golf* is extremely popular, though of course mainly among richer people; and in several towns the golf course has been cited to us as a prime example of a place where Protestant and Catholic meet in friendship. In both men's and women's golf the Republic and Northern Ireland play as one international side, though in the Ryder Cup, Walker Cup, and Curtiss Cup matches players from both North and South play in the 'Great Britain and Ireland' team.

9. *Swimming* also produces co-operation, including contests between Protestant and Catholic schools. There are separate water polo sides for the two parts of the country.

10. *Athletics* provide a continual source of dissension. In the early twenties the G.A.A. handed over control of athletics according to the Gaelic rules to the National Athletic and Cycling Association of Ireland. This body is under suspicion of using its claim to represent all Ireland as a vehicle of nationalist political propaganda; a cross-country cycle race at Limavady in 1959 was in consequence banned on the grounds that it might disturb the peace. The existence of separate rules for Gaelic athletic meetings produces a division between the activities of the two communities. The N.A.C.A. purports to represent its sport in the whole island, and in consequence it is not eligible to provide Olympic teams (which are picked from nations as defined by political boundaries). The Republic's Olympic team is provided by another body, the Amateur Athletic Union, which has good relations with the Northern Ireland Athletic Association.

11. *Boxing* is popular among Catholics, and successful boxers (whatever their religion) get warm support from all parts of the community.

It can be seen from this summary that, left to itself, sport in Northern Ireland does to some extent perform its traditional part as an influence for unity and friendship; but that where political and social factors are allowed to influence the organization of sport, it may help only to make the division between the communities more definite.

CHAPTER 11

CONCLUSIONS

In the Introduction we defined our purpose as being 'to look at the points of conflict and of co-operation in the dispassionate and impartial light of truth'. It is a feature of any long-continued quarrel on deeply-felt matters that the contestants tend to lose their sense of judgement, and to fight not the reality but a terrifying phantom created by their doubts and fears. There is, we think, in Northern Ireland a tendency to believe the worst of 'the other side', and a failure to make that leap of the imagination which is needed to see the other man's point of view. Perhaps this book will help some to understand that views different from their own can be both reasonable and deeply held, and that one can go much too far in attributing hardship to deliberate malice or discrimination.

But even when the divisions in the Northern Ireland community have been freed of all the accretions of emotional unreason, they remain real and profound. In Chapter 1 we have tried to sketch their historical origins; but it seems to us that it is impossible to find in the confused events of the past any answer to the problems of division in the present, save that a fuller knowledge of Irish history would help people to be more understanding and tolerant of the views of members of the other community. Chapter 3 shows how the religious division is related to the constitutional issue, and how the two together dominate the political life of the Province. This means that the actions of central and local government tend to be interpreted as the actions of a particular religious group. When a man in England is refused a Council house he may have bitter feelings towards his local Council, or perhaps towards 'Socialists' or 'Conservatives' in general; but in Northern Ireland he is quite likely to believe that the refusal is the result of a deliberate policy of unfairness to his religion.

In writing of social relations (Chapter 4) and of discrimination in employment (Chapter 6) we have tried to show how differences of national origin, segregation of housing areas, separate education and social life, and differences of economic status and opportunity act and interact so as to create a stable but deeply divided social structure. We would particularly stress the point of stability; it is extraordinary that a society should be so neatly balanced in so many respects. Even a difference in birth rates is offset, almost exactly, by a difference in emigration rates related to differences in economic opportunity. In forty years Northern Ireland has become much quieter and more settled, but little that is fundamental has changed; and indeed the divisions of society have in a few respects been made more secure and lasting by the growth and long acceptance of an institutional structure. For instance, a political system and area of government which were once considered by many to be too artificial to endure have grown to be accepted as a fact of life.

Nearly forty years ago, the feeling that nothing changes in the problems of Ireland was eloquently expressed by Sir Winston Churchill:

'Then came the great War. Every institution, almost, in the world was strained. Great Empires have been overturned. The whole map of Europe has been changed. The position of countries has been violently altered. The modes of thought of men, the whole outlook on affairs, the grouping of parties, all have encountered violent and tremendous changes in the deluge of the world. But as the deluge subsides and the waters fall short we see the dreary steeples of Fermanagh and Tyrone emerging once again. The integrity of their quarrel is one of the few institutions that has been unaltered in the cataclysm which has swept the world.'[1]

Those who read the speeches of Orangemen on the Twelfth of July, or hear Nationalist politicians talking about the Border, will be oppressed still by the same feeling of the eternal 'integrity of their quarrel'.

But it would be wrong to suppose that what has long existed will long continue. Great movements of opinion draw the Western world closer together, in matters of religion as well as of politics and economics. Before the threat that all civilized life may cease to exist upon the earth, the question of who may march along the Longstone Road loses something of its urgency. To a most notable degree, the interest of the people of the Republic of Ireland has turned away from a perpetual repetition of the events of 1916 and

[1] *Hansard*, 16 February 1922, col. 1270.

1921, and towards what is happening in the world outside. When Irish troops are fighting in the Congo, it is more difficult to take seriously the private armies whose battles consist of blowing up minor road bridges on the Border. This impact of world events is felt in Northern Ireland also, and will be felt much more. A new generation will have a different sense of what is important.

To say this is not to deny the reality of some of the grievances of the minority in Northern Ireland. We have tried in this book to set out the facts about them, and to show how the issues look from the point of view of the majority. Some complaints, for instance of discrimination, seem to us well founded; they are met by the doubtful argument, 'to do a great right do a little wrong'—that a moderate evil is justified to protect the greater good of the Protestant religion and the constitutional settlement. But other grievances are exaggerated, or show a lack of understanding of a reasonable opposing viewpoint; and sometimes there is a suspicion that those who complain of discrimination would in other circumstances be very ready to practise it themselves. We would like to see the exaggeration and lack of understanding fall away, and the issues reduced to a size and importance which are justified by the facts.

There is more in this book about conflict than about co-operation, because (despite all the bonds of individual friendship) there is at present more of separation than of unity in Northern Ireland society. Nevertheless, we have noted at a number of points how a common interest or enthusiasm, or some uniting influence of the local social structure, can transcend the general religious differences. Thus, the trade union movement (Chapter 9) is a uniting influence; many cultural activities, and certain games (Chapter 10), take no account of religion; the old social structure of the mountain farms, and the complex and diverse social life within the University, both provide opportunities for more natural relations between Protestant and Catholic. But a few such opportunities will not suffice. If Northern Ireland does not adapt herself to a world grown impatient of petty disunity, she will enter a period of increasing and painful stress.

The adaptation which is needed must come from both sides. A group of Presbyterian students has recently been trying to find out as much as possible about Roman Catholicism, by attending missions and inviting Catholics to speak to them. Such an attempt to understand one's neighbours is only common sense, but it would still be regarded by many as dangerous and unnecessary. The first change needed is that both Protestants and Catholics should be willing to learn more of the other's heritage and beliefs. We would, for instance, like to see non-Catholic schools take a lively interest in Irish history (objectively taught) and in Irish culture, so as to increase the area of life which is of common concern to all citizens.

We would also like to see a multiplication of opportunities for the two communities to join in common service and in common relaxation. Here Catholics have most to learn; we believe it to be neither right nor necessary for a great church, commanding the devotion of millions, to be so cautious in allowing its members to join in activities with Protestants. But attitudes are changing in other lands, and we hope that before long they will do the same in Ireland.

The tolerance between religions which we desire to see has been created in England because most people have become indifferent to the great issues of religion; but neither Protestant nor Catholic would wish to see Ulster take that path. Therefore there is no ultimate solution to be found except by learning the hard lesson that strong belief and Christian tolerance can exist together—and that it is possible to love your neighbour as yourself, even if you disagree with his beliefs. In the long run, the constitutional settlement and the Protestant religion cannot be protected by discrimination or the manipulation of small legal advantages, but only by actions and attitudes which are just and generous in intention. In the long run, those who put their trust in private military action, and those who take no trouble to understand the strong beliefs and valuable contribution of the Ulster Protestants, are bound to fail. Within some greater economic or even political unity of Western Europe, and within a Christian Church more conscious of its unity than of its divisions, both sides might realize what is valid in their desires, and the interaction of Protestant and Catholic might create a finer community than either could achieve by their own dominance.

POSTSCRIPT

CHARLES F. CARTER

In 1961, when Denis Barritt and I wrote the first edition of thi
book, we described Northern Ireland as having a 'stable bu
deeply divided social structure' (p. 153). In the light of wha
has followed, the word 'stable' may well seem ill-chosen. W
meant to imply that the divisions in the Province were self
perpetuating, and that there was no decided tendency toward
a change in the characteristics of the social (or political) system
But we did at that time hope that the ancient animosities and
rivalries would soften, and that the reforms initiated by Pope
John XXIII would open up new opportunities of co-operation
between the Churches. We noted that young people, in many
parts of the world, were impatient of the divisions of race o
religion or nationality created by their fathers. We hoped tha
some infection from this attitude would touch the younge
generation in Northern Ireland. We hoped also that the
influence of world events would turn the minds of Irish people
away from the trivial element in their quarrels. Of course
there remained grievances which were far from trivial; bu
much of the emotional conflict centred on matters such as the
holding of parades and the display of flags, which a less intro
spective community would long have recognized to b
unimportant, and even comic.

Our hopes were not simply wishful thinking. For severa
years there was indeed a growth of new forms of friendshi
and co-operation; and this has continued, though with littl
publicity, even during the present conflict. Without the bridge
thus built, the subsequent catastrophe would have been muc
greater. There were signs of a softening of political attitudes
which led to hopes of remedy for those grievances which wer
capable of being dealt with by political action. We were unde
no illusions that conflicts deeply rooted in history, and occur
ring in a nation which above all others is conscious of it
history, would subside in a short time. The possibility c
intensified conflict could certainly not be ruled out. But we di
not foresee the nature or the timing of the tragic events which
began in 1968.

Looking back, one can always see points at which the course of history might have been altered. I doubt, however, if it is a helpful exercise to isolate particular mistakes which have led to a national tragedy. The actors in the tragedy have seen themselves, at each point in time, as having little choice in what they did. No doubt this is because they lacked that power of statesmanship which overrides and commands events; but in the desperate realities of the situation, it is no help to long for a non-existent statesman to descend, a *deus ex machina*, and put things to rights. It is half a century since Winston Churchill drew attention to the continuing 'integrity' of the Irish quarrel (p. 153). I doubt if even his qualities would have been adequate to solve a problem so deep-seated. In this postscript, therefore, I do not apportion blame for what has happened: I seek only to explain it.

For the past half century, the state of Northern Ireland has been a Protestant supremacy. To the Unionist, this will appear as a somewhat loaded way of referring to the democratic right of a parliamentary majority to govern. But, of course, it is not the usual or intended result of the British type of democracy that a single party, representing an interest clearly defined by religious and social boundaries, should be permanently in power. The fact that this was occurring should have made us doubt the appropriateness of a simple parliamentary democracy for the government of a deeply divided community. As these words are written, means are being sought to give to the minority a share of power or entrenched rights; but the search comes half a century later than it should have done. In any case, the Protestant supremacy has been more than a permanent control of government. It has, as our book shows, implied a belief in a superior social position and a difference of economic status and opportunity. It has implied an *attitude* of superiority by the Protestant community which has allowed otherwise reasonable and intelligent men to acquiesce, over long periods, in forms of discrimination which were morally indefensible.

It was no answer to charges of discrimination to say that the Catholic community was equally ready to discriminate where it had power: that was the childish reply of 'you're another'.

Nor was it an answer to say that those who were not loyal subjects of the Queen should not have rights; for the people in question were not transients, on their way home to the Republic, but permanent residents, who had somehow to be won back from their state of disaffection. Indeed, the hollowness of many of the standard Unionist arguments in favour of 'things as they were' is shown by the speed with which the apparatus of discrimination was dismantled, under the combined influence of pressure from Westminster and a modicum of reforming zeal in parts of the Unionist Party.

But it is one thing to dismantle part of the framework of supremacy, and quite another to alter the attitude of mind which goes with it. It is now very evident that, whatever might be happening among the intelligentsia, there was not much shift of attitude among the Protestant working class and the farming community. The rise to fame of the Rev. Ian Paisley, while unquestionably related to his great gifts as a public speaker, showed also the great numbers of those who wanted to hear the traditional Unionist and Orange dogmas expressed with crude force and clarity. Indeed, for a considerable period many political commentators were disposed to assume that it was inevitable that, if an election to Stormont was held, the Rev. Paisley's adherents would emerge as rulers of the country.

So long as the Unionist Party remained in comfortable apathy, the equilibrium of the divided society could continue because it was familiar. As soon as there was talk of reform, the natural question in the minds of members of the Catholic minority was 'Is this a real change of attitude, or is it window-dressing, leaving everything important to go on as before?' For the informal expressions of the attitude of supremacy are much more important in everyday life than the explicit forms of discrimination which can be banned by legislation. For instance, experience in Britain shows that, despite legislation on race relations, employers are quite capable of perceiving good qualities in a white applicant for a job and missing the same qualities in a black applicant.

The evidence suggested that there was little change at the grass roots of Unionism: that, whatever Captain O'Neill might ay or do, the reality of what would happen would in the long un be nearer to what were then considered to be the wishes f the Rev. Paisley. It is, I suggest, this sense of being presented vith a false prospectus which explains the breaking of the long patience of the Catholic community. By 1968 and 1969, the continuation of the Protestant supremacy, though tolerated for so long, had become intolerable. I doubt if the break would have been made even then, if Northern Ireland had been economically successful. But she was involved in the general failure of British economic policies during the 1960s, aggravated by the division of responsibility between Stormont and Westminster. If there had been security of work, and the promise of prosperity, in Londonderry, Strabane, and Newry, and if Belfast had been less troubled by the uncertainties of the shipbuilding and aircraft industries, perhaps some now dead would be alive.

The equilibrium ended at a time when violent demonstrations, or violence in breaking up peaceful demonstrations, were common features in the news from many parts of the world. What happened may therefore owe something to the infection conveyed so quickly by the mass media from other countries, as well as to the memories of Ireland's own violent past. But the recourse to violence produced two inevitable results. One was the great intensification of division and hatred, and the growth of the 'war mentality' which sees justice and honour only on one's own side. The other was the deliberate exploitation and aggravation of the situation for political purposes.

Nevertheless, the path of events has not been predictable. In the early days it appeared that there would be mounting violence from both communities. It was in the context of a savage Protestant backlash that the British Army came to keep the peace, and was welcomed in Catholic areas as a friend and guardian. But then the Protestant community became much quieter. By 1971 the evidence of violence arose almost entirely from the guerrilla operations of the two wings of the Irish Republican Army, together with the stone throwing youths and children of the Catholic areas of Londonderry and Belfast. There were incidents (such as that at McGurk's Bar)

which might have been due to Protestant extremists, but in
the absence of any firm evidence could equally be ascribed
to careless handling of an I.R.A. bomb on the way to its
destination. Despite the presence in Northern Ireland of a
considerable number of newsmen anxious for copy, there was
not much published evidence of warlike preparation or activity
on the Protestant side, apart from the interest in rifle clubs
(which might indeed have serious implications for the future).
It would be naive to suppose that the Protestant community
had been converted to pacifism or felt secure under the pro
tection of the British Government; but, whatever lay behind
it, the Protestant passivity in 1970 and 1971 radically altered
the situation, by making the British Army appear to the
minority not as impartial guardians, but as oppressors of the
Catholic population and as servants of the Unionist Govern
ment. There are some who think that changes in Army policy
(or in the units employed) also had an effect in alienating the
Catholic community; and, of course, any large-scale use of
military force is liable to produce tragic and catastrophic events
such as the Londonderry killings in January 1972, which
confirm the impression of one-sidedness.

Seen in its mid-course, the Ulster conflict looked very differ
ent to different people. According to one view, it was an
enlarged version of earlier conflicts: a battle with small but
effective forces of the I.R.A., sustained by sympathizers in the
Republic and overseas, but gaining from the Catholic com
munity in Northern Ireland mainly the unwilling support of
those who feared retaliation if they failed to help. Therefore
(in this view), if the leaders could be captured and interned
no replacements would come forward, and the I.R.A. would
collapse: as peace was restored, co-operation with the Catholic
community would once again become possible: and it would
then be seen that the great and numerous measures of reform
had removed the grievances of the past, and laid a foundation
for happy relations in the future. It was unfortunate that British
inhibitions made it difficult to put down the armed insurrection
with the speed and finality which was desirable: but solid
progress was being made, information was flowing in, and time
would bring a final victory.

At the other extreme, the conflict was seen as a revolution, based on the general support of the Catholic community, with strong moral and material backing from outside the country. The first purpose of the revolution was to unite Ireland, whatever the view of the Protestants: the subsequent aims were various and unclear. The revolution would succeed when Britain conceded the case for a united Ireland (that is to say, went back on its promise in the Ireland Act, 1949, that Northern Ireland should not cease to be part of the United Kingdom without the consent of the Parliament of Northern Ireland; for the possibility of achieving unity by the re-entry of Southern Ireland to the United Kingdom could clearly be ruled out). Solid progress was being made—even to the point at which the Leader of the Opposition at Westminster had apparently conceded the case for a united Ireland. The right tactics for the Catholic side were seen to be to refuse all co-operation, to render a reformist policy ineffective, and to maintain a campaign of violence so as to demonstrate the impossibility of suppressing the I.R.A. Eventually the British would tire of spending blood and money on a cause for which they had no enthusiasm: they would abandon the Stormont Government, withdraw the Army, and the Protestants would then see the necessity of giving up their political, social, and economic power.

Between these views, there were of course many others. Some no doubt believed in the possibility of military victory over the I.R.A., but were quite unsure of how good relations with the minority could then be restored. Others, while seeing the final solution in terms of a united Ireland, certainly would not have used the term 'revolution', since they imagined the final government of Ireland as being very much like the Dublin Government of Mr. Lynch. The common feature of many of the expressions of opinion about the future course of events was, however, their lack of realism. It was not realistic to suppose that the I.R.A., in the period after the introduction of internment, was a small band of evil fanatics with no convinced support from the Catholic population. It has to be remembered that the I.R.A. factions were able, by their own choice of tactics, to provoke the authorities into countermeasures which strengthened I.R.A. support; for instance, by subjecting Catholic areas to brusque arms searches, or by putting in danger of injury or death Catholics who could be shown to be unconnected with the I.R.A. The military problem of suppressing the guerrilla movement was thus very difficult indeed—much worse than in earlier periods of unrest: and the cost of total military suppression seemed likely to be such a total breakdown of relations with the Catholic community (and, indeed, of civil government in Catholic areas) as to make it hard to see how good feeling could be restored.

The idea that the events of 1971 were stages in a revolution which was succeeding was, on the face of it, more plausible. It rested on the unflattering supposition that the British, under pressure from a guerrilla movement, would always back down on their promises. Yet those who assumed this underestimated the political difficulty of scrapping a promise to inhabitants of one's own country—quite a different matter from terminating colonial rule, which could be explained to the electorate as historically inevitable and morally virtuous. They also underestimated the problem of obtaining a collapse of the Protestant will to remain separate. A united Ireland containing a million unwilling Protestants would be as unstable and ungovernable as Northern Ireland had proved to be with half a million Catholics.

The greatest advantage won, up to the time of writing this postscript, by those who desired a united Ireland was the consequence of the re-introduction of internment, provoked by the campaign of violence. As our book makes clear (pp. 128–9), internment as an instrument of policy was nothing new, either in Northern Ireland or the Republic. The justification for using it had always been the lack of an alternative. It is not at all easy to bring political malefactors to justice in Ireland, even in normal times; and it was plainly moonshine to suppose that members of the I.R.A. who were caught could with any certainty be brought to account by the ordinary courts. Who would dare to give evidence against them? However, internment could be relied on to be a major provocation of the Catholic community, to lead even moderate Catholic opinion to a total rejection of the Stormont Government's policies, and to give sectors of British public opinion a moral reason for withholding support from Stormont.

The decision to go for internment was therefore a difficult one. It does not appear to have been taken under pressure from the Army; more probably it was simply a result of the struggle of Mr. Faulkner's Government to survive, being considered as a necessary *quid pro quo* for the banning of Protestant parades. But the operation was carried out in a ham-fisted way. In order to retain sympathy in Britain (which was essential to the Protestant cause) it was desirable to show that normal processes of law had broken down, but that the best available alternative processes were being used. In other words, it was desirable to charge those captured with an offence (whether actual participation in violence, or membership of an illegal organization), and to bring them before a court which, though necessarily abridging the rights of the accused and reaching verdicts on a lesser standard of proof than would be tolerated in peacetime, could be represented as the best 'rough justice' available. The emphasis should never have been allowed to rest on 'internment without trial', but on the quality of the legal review procedure which would be adopted in each case.

Having lost this psychological battle, the authorities, with a singular lack of imagination and intelligence, allowed certain of the internees to be subjected to the procedures for questioning described in the Compton Report. These procedures were, in any ordinary vocabulary, brutal; the attempt to define them otherwise was certain to appear as a quibble. A significant part of the British public considered that brutality to one's enemies was fully justifiable; some others may have been convinced by the argument that the evil was justified by the information obtained. But there is little doubt that the overall effect of being found out in acts of deliberate brutality was a serious blow to the Protestant side. Yet it was inevitable that the acts *would* be found out, and that skilled use of them would be made in propaganda. The only way of concealing brutal treatment would have been to ensure that no internee was released, and no visitors of any kind allowed to go to an internment camp— not even the Red Cross.

There are different views about whether internment, on balance, was justified. In my judgement it was not, for it closed so many doors to solutions of the Ulster problem other than the extreme ones—total military victory, or a united Ireland. But it was one thing to say that one would have advised Mr. Faulkner not to seek internment in the form adopted: and quite another to advise the reversal of the policy, once adopted. The problem of doing this was to find a way out which was not simply a capitulation to the I.R.A. (of a kind which would be likely to arouse a violent reaction on the Protestant side).

Whereas our book represents the Northern Ireland problem as a largely internal affair, a quarrel to be resolved by Ulstermen, the position at the time of writing this postscript (January 1972)[1] is that the immediate future of the conflict depends, not only on opinions and emotions in Ireland as a whole, but also (and largely) on the British Government and British public opinion: that is, on the resolution with which the British Army is used to obtain a military victory over the guerrillas, and the willingness or unwillingness of public opinion to contemplate a break-up of the United Kingdom and the creation of a united Ireland. This is an unfortunate development. Two generations in Britain have been able to forget the Irish problem, with the inevitable result that most people are ignorant of its history and nature. The Southern Irish are indeed a familiar part of British life, as inhabitants of a foreign country who nevertheless enjoy a super-Commonwealth status and come over in considerable numbers to find jobs. But one does not achieve an understanding of Irish politics, or Irish nationalist fanaticism, by meeting Irishmen on building sites. Furthermore, Ulstermen are much less known and understood in Britain, except in a few places with an Orange tradition. The English perhaps most often regard them as unlovable bigots. This is not a situation in which it is desirable that Britain should have to make decisions crucial to the future of Ireland. The danger of wrong decisions (or of the inaction which can be as dangerous as wrong action) is increased by the division of responsibility between the Governments at Westminster and Stormont, and by the fact that the Stormont Government has very little room for manoeuvre between the demands of the British Government for progress towards reform and the fears of its traditional supporters.

[1] Slightly revised in March 1972.

The reader of this postscript will have the benefit of hindsight as to what has happened during the time of publication. There may have been new disasters and new suffering, or new and hopeful initiatives and a growth of moderation and sanity. But the Ulster problem will not have been 'solved'. The scars of conflict are carried by the memory, and it will be many long years before the experiences of recent years cease to influence men's actions. It is not easy for the English to recognize the power of memory in Ireland. Today's schoolchildren in England do not, so far as I can observe, have any animosity towards Germans; the bitterness of two world wars has left no trace. It comes as a surprise, therefore, to hear Irish people quoting much older events as though they were living grievances.

If the power of memory is to be curbed, and hatred is to die away, it will be urgently necessary to find a settlement in which members of the two communities can meet each other more freely and take part in common action. So long as Protestants and Catholics live apart, learn apart, work apart, and find their relaxations apart, there will be a growth of evil rumour about 'the other side', unchecked by a recognition of common humanity. This need for the communities to get to know each other means that we must classify as unsatisfactory and temporary any outcome of the present conflict which is seen, either as a victory of one side over the other, or as a confirmation of 'apartheid'. The defeated side would almost certainly withdraw behind its mental barriers, and the hatred would remain to cause future trouble.

Therefore neither a British abandonment of the Protestant cause, leading to a united Ireland, nor a continuing Protestant supremacy consequent upon a temporary military defeat of the I.R.A., can be regarded as desirable solutions. It is conceivable that the conflict will in fact end in stalemate because of war-weariness, and that the two communities may recognize the impossibility of continuing with past bigotry and enmity. But it would be better if the end came, not in desperation, but in the hope born of a new idea. In what direction should such an idea be sought?

The modification of attitudes requires a readiness in ordinary men to abandon familiar ideas, and cannot be achieved by political institutions alone. Nevertheless, the right political institutions, accompanied by strong leadership, can set an example for personal attitudes. As I have suggested above, it has too easily been assumed that the British form of parliamentary democracy is necessarily appropriate: that is, government answerable to a House of Commons, with only a slight check from the second chamber (the House of Lords or Senate). Changes such as the use of proportional representation have been considered, but in practice this would make little difference.

What is needed is bolder constitutional thinking, starting from a declaration of principle as to what is to be achieved. This declaration should have two parts. First, there must be an end of the Protestant supremacy, in so far as it is embodied in or supported by the forms of government. Second, there must be no place in Ulster for a romantic Catholic-Irish nationalism which regards the descendants of seventeenth, eighteenth, and nineteenth century immigrants as aliens or second-class citizens. (At its better moments, Irish nationalism has been non-sectarian.) The constitution must therefore give a share of effective power to both communities, and should probably provide that some things can only be done by agreement of representatives of both communities. It must not be capable of being subverted so as to become an instrument of domination of one group over the other. There has been no lack of people who have wanted to see a political initiative: but, particularly within Ireland, there has been a nervousness about entering into hard discussion of specific proposals which might stand a chance of acceptance in both communities. The reason for this is that, in a situation of deep division, almost every proposal has been seen to favour one side or the other: and has then been automatically condemned by the other side, without attention to its real merits. The path of prudence, therefore, has been to advance good ideas secretly, not exposing them to attack until absolutely necessary. There is evidence that many interesting suggestions have been quietly discussed in London, Dublin, or Belfast. The examples which follow (accompanied by some personal comments) may serve to illustrate some of the possibilities.

It has been argued by some that the carrying out of principles such as I have stated above could be made easier if the powers of government in Northern Ireland were taken over by an appointed Commission for a period of (say) three to five years. Such a Commission could have regard to moderate and responsible opinion in both communities; it could carry out further irreversible reforms; and, in a period of peace and new co-operation, the framework of Ulster politics might be changed, so that at the end of the period ordinary forms of parliamentary democracy could be re-introduced but with a quite new and non-sectarian structure of parties.

In fact, in March 1972 rule by a minister from London (Mr. Whitelaw) with an advisory Commission became necessary, because of a breakdown of relations with the Stormont Government (see p. xxviii). But to regard this as a means to a *solution* seems to me to involve too many 'ifs'. The suspension of all forms of representation (at provincial level) must properly be for a limited period: during that period new political growth *may* occur, but equally there may be a retreat to the old battle lines, with the intention of renewing sectarian combat, at Stormont or elsewhere, as soon as possible.

A more fundamental reform has been proposed, embodying the suggested two principles, namely to have a genuine two-chamber system (that is, one in which the Senate has strong powers to thwart the House of Commons), and to entrench the position of the minority in determining the composition of the Senate. There would then have to be, as in the American system, joint committees to iron out differences of view between the chambers. There would, of course, be a danger of deadlock; but deadlocks are inconvenient, and tend to be resolved. However, this proposal may be too simple, in that it does not deal with the other great problem of Ulster government—the extent of the devolution of power from Westminster.

At one extreme, if *all* central government powers reverted to Westminster (so that Northern Ireland became a collection of local authorities) it would seem inevitable that areas which desired to should be allowed to secede to the Republic: so that Northern Ireland would become smaller, with a somewhat greater proportion of Protestants, but with a considerable remaining Catholic minority. The rights of this minority could be entrenched in the structure of local government, but otherwise would depend on the wisdom of the British Government.

This, however, is a solution which would probably evoke universal hostility. Now if Northern Ireland, whether within its present boundaries or within modified boundaries, is to have some 'central government' powers, these should (in my view) include the key decisions of economic policy. No doubt it is necessary to seek economic *aid* from Britain, but this does not mean that rates of taxation or of social benefits have to be identical. The economic prospects of the province as a peripheral and heavily subsidized depressed area in the United Kingdom are not good; and, in the context of the European Economic Community, it might be better to try to negotiate some sort of privileged status such as that claimed by the Republic of Ireland. If that is not available, it would nevertheless be better that the province should make its own choice on alignment to British (or, for that matter, to Republic of Ireland) economic policy.

If, then, the role of Westminster were to be confined largely[2] to defence and foreign policy (thus putting the maximum possible amount of power into provincial or community hands), it has been suggested that these functions might be the subject of a *condominium* with the Republic, citizens of Northern Ireland being allowed to opt for either nationality, and to vote for both Parliaments. For the part of foreign policy most significant to a province, namely trade policy, will already be subject to standardization under the E.E.C.; Britain and Ireland should be able to agree about defence against external aggression against Ireland itself, North or South: and the reserve power of using defence forces for police purposes would be much more acceptable if it were a joint function. The Northern Ireland constitution should, of course, be constructed so as to

---

[2] The other excepted and reserved matters (i.e. not controlled by Stormont) included such things as regulation of merchant shipping and of aerial navigation, the coinage, weights and measures, and patent rights, which should be capable of being covered by *ad hoc* arrangements. The Post Office is now a commercial service. The Supreme Court might be made an instrument of the *condominium*.

entrench the position of both communities, and thus to assure basic human rights.

These are merely examples of the kind of thinking needed if Northern Ireland is to have a constitution which reflects the attitudes which it is desirable to foster in the divided society, and which acknowledges both the loyalty of the Protestant community to the British Crown and the sense of Irish 'belonging' in the Catholic community. Our hope, in reissuing this book, is to encourage that understanding of the underlying problems which is necessary if timely and imaginative long-term solutions are to be proposed and worked out with thoroughness and attention to detail.

INDEX